Fruit and Vegetable Consumption Links to Depression Symptoms

Aurora Obama

Copyright © [2023]

Author: **Aurora Obama**

Title: **Fruit and Vegetable Consumption Links to Depression Symptoms**

All rights reserved. No part of this book may be reproduced or transmitted in any form or by any means, electronic or mechanical, including photocopying, recording, or by any information storage and retrieval system, without permission in writing from the author.

This book is a product of [Publisher's **Aurora Obama**

ISBN:

ABSTRACT

Depression is a highly recurrent, chronic, and potentially lifelong mental illness. Increasing efforts to develop preventive strategies for depression is a critical investment. The role of diet and particularly higher fruit and vegetable consumption has been of particular interest as a novel approach to reduce the risk of depression. However, the associations between fruit and vegetable consumption and depression symptoms remain largely unexplored in young people and adults.

This book comprises two studies, a systematic review[1] and a secondary analysis study[1]. The first study aimed to systematically review the longitudinal studies of the associations between fruit and vegetable consumption and depression symptoms in young people and adults aged 15-45. The second study examined the differential effects of fruit and vegetables in relation to depression symptoms over a 15-year follow-up in young women from the 1973–78 cohort of the Australian Longitudinal Study on Women's Health (ALSWH).

Findings from the systematic review suggested that a possible association exists between fruit and vegetable consumption and depression symptoms, particularly consuming fruit on a daily basis. The secondary analysis supported the evidence that fruit and vegetable consumption was cross-sectionally associated with lower odds of depression symptoms over 15 years of follow-up. In longitudinal analysis, higher intake of fruit ($\geq$ 4 servings) and vegetable ($\geq$ 5 servings) was consistently associated with lower odds of depressive symptoms, with a 25% lower odds (OR 0.75; 95% CI 0.57, 0.97; p = 0.031) and a 19% lower odds (OR 0.81; 95% CI 0.70, 0.94; p = 0.007) than consuming one serve or less of fruit and vegetable respectively.

---

[1] This book is presented as a non-traditional research book by publication format as outlined by Macquarie University Higher Degree Research Unit. This format necessitates the preparation of paper which may be submitted for publication. This structure necessitates some repetition between papers.

The collective book findings highlight the importance of consuming adequate fruit and vegetables for reducing the risk of depression symptoms. Therefore, increasing fruit and vegetable consumption can be a promising approach for reducing the risk of depression symptoms. Furthermore, policy actions at a national and international level are needed to increase the availability, acceptability and affordability of fruit and vegetables.

TABLE OF CONTENTS

ABSTRACT ....
TABLE OF CONTENTS ....
LIST OF FIGURES ....
LIST OF ABBREVIATIONS ....

Chapter 1: Introduction... 15
   Introduction 15
   Key terms and definitions in depression.. 16
   Disease burden of depression 17
      The recent global burden 17
      Gender differences in depression 18
      Depression in young people and adults 19
   Economic cost of depression and mental disorders... 20
   Aetiology and risk factors for depression.. 20
      Genetic and biological factors 21
      Adverse life events 21
      Lifestyle factors 22
   Treatment approaches for depression 23
   Preventive approaches for depression 24
   Role of a healthy diet to reduce the risk of depression.. 25
   Fruit and vegetables as a promising approach to prevent depression........................ 25
   Trends in fruit and vegetable consumption and dietary guidelines 27
   book rationale... 28
   book objectives.. 29
   book overview... 29
   References 31
Chapter 2: 41

Study 1: Association between fruit and vegetable consumption and depression symptoms in young people and adults aged 15-45: a systematic review of cohort studies 41

    Rationale for the systematic review 41

    Article content 42

    Publication systematic review 43

        Abstract 43

        Introduction 43

        Materials and methods 45

        Results 46

        Discussion 54

        Conclusions 57

        Appendix A 58

        References 58

    Implications for the future research 63

    References 64

Chapter 3: 66

Study 2: Fruit and vegetable consumption and depression symptoms in young women: results from 1973-78 cohort of the Australian Longitudinal Study on Women's Health 66

    Rationale for the secondary analysis 66

    Article content 67

    Fruit and vegetable consumption and depression symptoms in young women: results from 1973–78 cohort of the Australian Longitudinal Study on Women's Health 68

        Abstract 69

        Introduction 70

        Methodology 71

        Results 76

        Discussion 79

        Conclusion 83

        Supplementary material 83

        Declarations 84

        References 85

    Further information 94

    References 95

Chapter 4: Discussion and Conclusion 96

    Key findings from this research 96

Summary of systematic review findings 96
Summary of the 1973–78 cohort of the ALSWH findings.. 97
Contribution of the two studies to the literature 97
Strengths and limitation... 99
Future research directions... 100
    Gender differences... 100
    Differences in assessment of depression 101
    Differences in measurement of fruit and vegetable intake 101
    Reverse causality 101
Implications for the prevention of depression 101
Conclusion and contribution to policy, practice, and research 103

LIST OF FIGURES

Figure 1. A comparison of the incident cases of depression at a regional level in 1990 (left) and 2017 (right). Taken from: Liu Q et al. Changes in the global burden of depression from 1990 to 2017: Findings from the Global Burden of Disease study. Journal of psychiatric research. 2020;126:134–40. doi: 10.1016/j.jpsychires.2019.08.002. 18

Figure 2. Potential mechanisms of diet, sleep and physical activity on MDD. Taken from: Lopresti AL, Hood SD, Drummond PD. A review of lifestyle factors that contribute to important pathways associated with major depression: diet, sleep and exercise. Journal of affective disorders. 2013;148(1):12–27. Doi: 10.1016/j.jad.2013.01.014. 23

LIST OF ABBREVIATIONS

5HT	5-hydroxytryptamine
AHEI	Alternate healthy eating index
ALSWH	Australian Longitudinal Study on Women's Health
BMI	Body Mass Index
BH4	Tetrahydrobiopterin
CESD	Center for Epidemiologic Studies Depression Scale
CI	Confidence interval
CIDI-SF	Composite International Diagnostic Interview-Short Form
DALYs	Disability-adjusted life years
Dep	Depression
Dis	Distress
DSM-5	Diagnostic and Statistical Manual of Mental Disorders
GEE	Generalised estimating equations
GHQ-12	General Health Questionnaire-12
HR	Hazard ratio
J-MICC	Japan Multi-Institutional Collaborative Cohort
K6	Kessler psychological distress scale
MCS	Mental component summary
MDD	Major depressive disorder
MDP	Mediterranean dietary pattern
MET	Metabolic equivalent
MFQ	Moods and Feelings Questionnaire
MICE	Multivariate imputation by chained equations
MHI-5	5-item Mental health index
NOS	Newcastle-Ottawa Scale
NS	Not significant
OR	Odds ratio
PNNS-GS	French Programme National Nutrition Sante'-Guidelines Score
PROSPERO	International Prospective Register of Systematic Reviews

Q	Quartile/quintile
RCT	Randomised controlled trial
RCGHA	Research Centre for Gender, Health, and Ageing
Ref	Reference
SAMe	S-adenosylmethionine
SD	Standard deviation
SF-12	12-Item Short Form Health Survey
SPHC	Stockholm Public Health Cohort
SU.VI.MAX	The Supplementation en Vitamines et Mineraux Antioxydants
UK	United Kingdom
UKHLS	UK Household Longitudinal Study
USA	United States of America
WHO	World Health Organization

Chapter 1: Introduction

Introduction

Depression is a highly recurrent, chronic, and potentially lifelong mental illness linked to diminished social functioning and can adversely affect the quality of life.(1-3) Major depressive disorder (MDD) is the most common mental disorder in most societies worldwide, with 264 million people suffering from this disorder in 2017.(4) Due to the often recurrent course, this disorder can significantly impact daily activities, such as social interaction and work productivity.(5)

Depression has been identified as a major contributor to global disability,(4) particularly in the young population aged 10-49.(6) The percentage change in the number of disability-adjusted life years (DALYs) between 1990 and 2019 in depressive symptoms has risen dramatically in those aged 10-24 and aged 25-49, an increase of 20.7% and an increase of 53.2%, respectively.(6) As a consequence, the annual costs of depression are tremendous and make depression a substantial economic burden for countries.(7-9)

The current trends indicate that more rapid increases in depression prevalence occurred among young populations,(10) yet they are less likely to seek any treatments, which means these trends translate into a growing number of young people with untreated depression.(11) An increasing and alarming trend in incident cases of depression, particularly in young people and adults, emphasises the importance of preventing the onset of mental disorders. Increasing efforts to develop and implement feasible preventive interventions for depression is a critical investment to reduce the incidence of depression and associated disability in the population.(12) Hence, preventing the onset of depression has become a global priority for public health intervention.

Key terms and definitions in depression

Depression refers to conditions where individuals experience persistent low moods and a lack of interest in enjoyable activities.(13) According to the Diagnostic and Statistical Manual of Mental Disorders edition 5th (DSM-5), MDD is characterised by "discrete episodes of at least two weeks' duration (although most episodes last considerably longer) involving clear-cut changes in affect, cognition, and neurogenerative functions and inter-episode remission".(14) The criterion symptoms for MDD present during the same 2-week interval with a minimum of five of the following symptoms significant weight loss, insomnia, fatigue nearly every day, feelings of worthlessness, diminished ability to concentrate, recurrent suicidal ideation, and at least either depressed mood (e.g., feels empty, sad, hopeless) or loss of interest or pleasure.(14) MDD is also referred to as clinical depression which has been assessed by mental health professionals.

Adequate identification of depression during the screening phase is crucial for treatment and referral to mental health professionals.(15) Self-report and clinical interview are the main instruments to assess depression severity. Various reliable and validated rating scales for depressive symptoms are available, such as the Beck Depression Inventory,(16) the Center for Epidemiologic Studies Depression Scale (CES-D),(17) the Patient Health Questionnaire,(18) and the Hamilton Rating Scale for Depression.(19) These rating scales are short self-report scales designed for depression screening in primary care settings and extensively used for research in the general population. Individuals complete a scale using multiple-choice response formats to indicate whether depression symptoms are present over a certain period. Then, a validated cut of scores has been recommended on each scale to determine depression severity.

Some key terms are closely related to depression, such as mental disorders and subjective well-being. According to DSM-5, "a mental disorder is a syndrome characterised by clinically significant disturbance in an individual's cognition, emotion regulation, or behaviour that reflects a dysfunction in the psychological, biological, or developmental processes underlying mental functioning."(14)

Depression is widely known as one of the common mental disorders along with anxiety disorders because these disorders are highly prevalent in the population.(20) In past decades, a large number of studies have been conducted to investigate the relationship between well-being and depression.(21-24) To date, there is no decisive definition of well-being; however, subjective well-being generally includes a sense of fulfilment, life satisfaction, and positive functioning.(25-27) Individuals who frequently experience negative emotions such as depressed mood are more likely to have a low level of subjective well-being.(27)

Disease burden of depression

The recent global burden

Depression alone has the largest effect on decrements in health than other chronic diseases, such as diabetes, angina, and asthma.(10) According to World Health Organization (WHO), this debilitating disorder was the single largest contributor to global disability in 2015 (20) and is expected to be the leading cause of disease burden globally by 2030.(28) In the past few decades, there is evidence that both the incidence and prevalence of depression has increased worldwide.(1, 10, 29-33) A recent study analysing the trends in depression indicated that depression incidence globally increased significantly by almost 50% between 1990 and 2017.(1) Figure 1 depicts a comparison of the incident cases of depression at a regional level in 1990 and 2017. In a systematic review and meta-analysis study, Moreno-Agostino et al.(33) suggested a predominant increasing trend in the prevalence of depression in the general population over time. The lifetime prevalence of depression among adults in the communities from 30 countries was nearly 11% between 1994 and 2014.(2) Furthermore, this study also found significant gender differences in depression prevalence, with a higher likelihood of depression in women.(2)

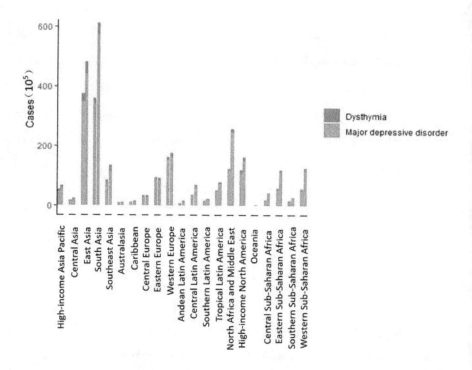

Figure 1. A comparison of the incident cases of depression at a regional level in 1990 (left) and 2017 (right). Taken from: Liu Q et al. Changes in the global burden of depression from 1990 to 2017: Findings from the Global Burden of Disease study. Journal of psychiatric research. 2020;126:134–40. doi: *10.1016/j.jpsychires.2019.08.002*.[2]

Gender differences in depression

Gender differences in depression have been observed, where women are twice as likely to develop depression than men during their lifetime.(34, 35) Moreover, depressive disorders were the second leading cause of DALYs among women after gynaecological disorders.(6) Findings from The Singapore Mental Health Study highlighted that women have a higher lifetime prevalence of MDD than men.(36) A higher lifetime prevalence may be explained by that women reported a younger age

---

[2] This article is published under the terms of the Creative Commons Attribution-NonCommercial-No Derivatives License (CC BY NC ND) https://creativecommons.org/licenses/by-nc-nd/4.0/

of onset of MDD than men.(37) Regarding the severity of depression, no difference was observed between women and men.(37)

A meta-analysis showed that women are more likely to suffer from major depression than men.(38) These disparities may be attributable to neurobiological, immune, and transcriptional signatures from a lens of biological sex.(39) Similarly, a recent systematic review suggested different biological patterns for women and men with MDD, such as monoaminergic system, immune system, and neuroplasticity.(40) It should be noted that the phenomenon may also be dependent on the type of depression,(41) sociocultural,(42) stress exposure and stress processes.(43)

Depression in young people and adults

A number of studies have concluded that the first onset of depressive episode and the peak age of first-lifetime MDD onset typically occurs in the 20s to early 30s, which is the period of life transition in adulthood.(44-47) A longitudinal study in Norway showed that MDD is highly prevalent among young adults in their twenties, with the prevalence in the past year ranging from 8.3% to 12.4%.(47) In alignment with this study, findings from the National Survey on Drug Use and Health in the United States reported young adults aged 18-25 years have the highest rates of major depressive episode (13.1%) compared with other age groups.(48)

A similar trend is also observed in Australia, with a significant increase in major depression among younger people. The South Australian Health Omnibus surveys found a substantial increase in the prevalence of major depression from 6.8% to 10.3% between 1998 and 2008.(49) Similarly, the proportion of Australians who had depression or feelings of depression increased from 8.9% in 2014–15 to 10.4% in 2017-18.(50) To date, suicide and mental disorders were the leading causes of total burden in Australia among people aged 15-44, according to Australia's health 2020 report.(51) The latest Productivity Commission Inquiry Report highlighted the urgency of early prevention in mental disorders because the onset of the first mental disorder occurs before the age of 21 years.(52)

Economic cost of depression and mental disorders

The high prevalence of mental disorders is expected to incur extensive costs to individuals, families, and society. The cumulative economic output loss in mental disorders is projected to be US$ 16.3 trillion worldwide between 2011 and 2030.(53) Furthermore, the estimated average annual economic loss associated with anxiety and depression is US$ 1 trillion worldwide.(54) In Australia, the budget for mental health services increased from AU$ 5.3 billion in 2004–5 to AU$ 10.6 billion in 2018–19.(8) Similarly, the cost of depression-associated including increased health service and drug prescriptions in the United Kingdom is estimated at £11 billion annually.(9) Among the most costly medical conditions in the USA was mental disorders, with spending surpassing US$200 billion in 2013.(7)

Apart from these direct costs, indirect costs associated with mental disorders due to lost productivity and labour force participation are also extensive. For example, a study in Pakistan revealed that nearly 60% of the economic burden of mental disorders was attributable to productivity losses, while 37% was attributable to medical care costs.(55) Likewise, indirect costs for depression in China represented about 84% of the total estimated cost of depression.(56) For these reasons, the tremendous annual costs associated with mental disorders, depression in particular, have contributed to a substantial economic burden for countries.

Aetiology and risk factors for depression

Despite continued research in understanding the aetiology and pathophysiological of depression, the precise mechanisms leading to the development of depression remain unclear.(57) The complex nature of depression makes it an etiologically heterogeneous disorder with possible pathways that have been linked to biological predisposition, adverse life events, and lifestyle choices.(58)

Genetic and biological factors

Existing family and twin studies have shown substantial evidence that heritability plays an important role in severe forms of depression.(57, 59, 60) A meta-analysis estimated that heritability has contributed to depression, ranging from 31% to 42% (59), and women have a higher heritability of liability to major depression than men.(60) In order to elucidate its aetiology, multiple neurobiological studies have postulated possible pathophysiological mechanisms of depression in past decades.(9, 61-67) A prominent hypothesis of depression called the monoamine hypothesis proposed a functional deficiency of monoamine neurotransmitters, such as 5-hydroxytryptamine (5HT) or serotonin, norepinephrine, and dopamine, which result in decreased neurotransmission and impaired cognitive function, which may increase susceptibility to depression.(9) Moreover, an alteration in 5HT signalling led to fewer 5HT uptake sites on platelets that may predict suicidality.(61) Evidence from existing monoamine studies demonstrates that monoaminergic systems are instrumental to many behavioural symptoms of depression, such as reduced motivation, low mood, and fatigue.(68, 69)

Adverse life events

Stressful life events are a major risk factor for depression. It has been generally observed that the experience of loss and grief is substantially associated with a higher risk of depression.(70-73) Existing evidence shows that exposure to adverse life events at a younger age can lead to depressive exacerbation.(74-76) Adult depression may also be triggered by a single specific experience at a younger age. For instance, individuals experiencing childhood sexual or emotional abuse are more likely to develop adult depression, especially among women.(77-80)

Regarding the developmental stage, Arnett et al.(81, 82) argued that emerging adulthood is considered as a distinct period of the lifespan, where most emerging adults experience stressful events based on life transitions. Much of the instability in emerging adulthood stems from relationships, work, identity explorations (81, 82). One of the consequences of these life events, emerging adults often feeling depressed (81), which may put them at increased risk for developing depression.(83)

Lifestyle factors

A large and growing body of literature has attempted to explain the relationship between depression and unhealthy lifestyles, such as poor diet,(84-86) lack of physical activity,(84, 87, 88) sleep deprivation,(89, 90) heavy drinking,(87, 91, 92) and smoking.(87, 93, 94) Accumulating evidence suggests that these factors are behavioural determinants of depression.(84, 86-88, 91, 95, 96) More recent attention has focused on changes in diet, sleep, and physical activity concurrently with the change in the prevalence of depression.

A longitudinal study from the Personality and Total Health project highlighted that long term exposure to unhealthy dietary patterns predisposed an individual to depression over the lifespan.(97) A community-based cohort study in Texas found that sleep deprivation was associated with an increased risk of major depression among adolescents.(89) Similarly, a population-based study in Canada reported that physical inactivity was associated with an increased likelihood of depression symptoms among youth.(88) Although these results need to be interpreted with caution due to the potential reverse causality, a possible pathway is that poor diet, impaired sleep, and reduced physical activity may influence several biological processes related to major depression in the nervous system (see Figure 2).(90)

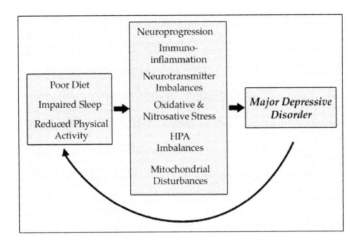

Figure 2. Potential mechanisms of diet, sleep and physical activity on MDD. Taken from: Lopresti AL, Hood SD, Drummond PD. A review of lifestyle factors that contribute to important pathways associated with major depression: diet, sleep and exercise. Journal of affective disorders. 2013;148(1):12–27. Doi: *10.1016/j.jad.2013.01.014*.[3]

Treatment approaches for depression

An individual treatment approach is the most common intervention to cure depression, with pharmacotherapy and psychotherapy as primary treatments.(98) It is widely known that antidepressant drugs are frequently used to treat patients with MDD, which are available worldwide.(99) However, most common antidepressants may cause side effects, which may affect medication adherence among patients.(100) Although extensive research has been undertaken on the efficacy and effectiveness of antidepressants, valid evidence for long-term antidepressant treatment is somewhat controversial and lacking.(101, 102)

A number of psychotherapies for depression have been developed and tested in mental health care over the last decades. Cognitive-behavioural therapy is one of the most common psychotherapies

---

[3] Available under a license obtained from the Journal of Affective Disorders for republish of a portion (figure/table/illustration) in a book/book; order date: 25-Jun-2021; Order license ID: 5096231276935.

for depression in a primary care setting aimed at cognitive restructuring for patients with mild-to-moderate depressive episodes.(103, 104) A meta-analysis showed a positive impact on the quality of life of patients with depression after receiving psychotherapy.(105) However, the proportion of individuals who receive appropriate treatment is lower than 50%.(106) The WHO World Mental Health surveys indicated that the proportion of people with depressive disorder receiving minimally adequate treatment was very low (16.5%).(107) Current treatments under optimal conditions potentially avert only one-third of the disease burden associated with MDD.(108)

Preventive approaches for depression

Several studies suggest that preventive interventions can be a promising approach to further reducing the global burden of depression by reducing the risk or delaying the onset of depression.(98, 108, 109) However, despite positive progress on mental health services, the prevention of depression remains a neglected part of global efforts. Previous meta-analyses of psychological interventions showed evidence that currently available interventions can prevent depressive disorders between 19% and 38% in high-risk individuals of all ages.(98, 108, 110)

Another emerging area with potential is lifestyle approaches for depression prevention. Several reviews suggest lifestyle modification may play a crucial role in preventing and treating mental disorders, including depression.(90, 111, 112) In recent years, there has been an increasing amount of literature on dietary and exercise interventions in relation to depression. Recent systematic reviews indicate that interventions that involve exercise might have a modest effect on reducing depressive symptoms.(113, 114) Similarly, growing nutritional studies examining the effects of a healthy diet on depressive symptoms have yielded positive results. Preliminary evidence suggested maintaining a healthy diet may be a promising approach to preventing depression.(115)

Role of a healthy diet to reduce the risk of depression

Healthy diets are widely recognised as being linked with better physical and mental health status.(116-118) The emerging findings show that dietary modifications may provide substantial benefits for some neurological conditions.(119, 120) Several systematic reviews of diet-depression studies have concluded that adhering to healthy dietary patterns are associated with a reduced risk of depressive symptoms.(121-123) A recent narrative review suggests that the Mediterranean and traditional diets have an inverse association with the incidence of depression in adolescents.(124) A randomised controlled trial confirmed that a brief healthy diet intervention following Mediterranean-style diets was significantly associated with lower depressive symptoms in young adults.(125) A meta-analysis shows that healthy diet interventions had a positive effect on depression symptoms, despite the small numbers, with the majority of studies in older populations.(126) It is worth noting that most dietary interventions in this meta-analysis comprised of higher fruit and vegetable consumption. The possible pathway to elucidate the association between higher adherence to a healthy diet and a lower risk of depression is the role of B_{12}, folic acid, and magnesium in nervous system functions.(115, 127, 128)

Fruit and vegetables as a promising approach to prevent depression

According to WHO,(129) it is estimated that up to 3.9 million deaths were attributable to insufficient intake of fruit and vegetables in 2017. The Global Burden of Disease Study 2017 revealed that low consumption of fruit and vegetables was the leading dietary risk factor for mortality and DALYs globally.(129) Each component accounted for more than 2% of global mortality.(129) Low fruit and vegetable consumption has been linked to increased risk of chronic diseases,(130-132) body weight and obesity.(133, 134) It has also been associated with common mental disorders, such as depression and anxiety.(135, 136) To date, most adults consume less than the recommended daily servings of fruit and vegetables, which may increase their risk to develop a range of non-communicable diseases (137) and mental disorders over time.(138)

Previous systematic reviews found that certain food groups may be associated with reduced depression risk. Most of the reviews suggest the role of fruit and vegetables in the development of depression.(139-142) For example, a systematic review evaluating the association between the Mediterranean diet and depression reported that greater adherence to dietary patterns characterised by higher intakes of fruit and vegetable is associated with a lower risk of depression.(122) Another review of dietary patterns and depression in community-dwelling adults also showed fruit and vegetables represent a "beneficial" component to lower the risk of depression.(121) Given these findings, specific food groups may drive the association between a healthy diet and depression symptoms. Notably, fruit and vegetables may have a particular role in relation to depression than other food groups. Therefore, studies examining a specific food group provide further evidence of whether the association between a healthy diet and depression symptoms are driven by single foods or few key food groups.

Some studies showed that higher fruit and vegetable consumption was associated with reduced odds of depressive symptoms,(135, 143, 144) whereas the association was not observed in other studies.(145-147) Furthermore, some studies examining the association in women populations indicate a potentially role of fruit and vegetable in lowering the risk of depression symptoms.(148, 149) A plausible mechanism has been proposed that fruit and vegetables are rich in minerals, vitamins, antioxidants, which might be beneficial to protect against depression.(141, 142, 150) Recent systematic reviews indicated that increased fruit and vegetable consumption might protect against depression development in adults, but many were conducted in older populations.(151, 152) Additionally, the majority of findings from observational studies on the association of fruit and vegetable consumption and depression symptoms were also drawn from older populations. It is a plausible explanation of inconsistencies observed that health conditions, such as chronic diseases, may act as confounders in this association, notably in older populations. Moreover, it is acknowledged that most findings from previous systematic reviews were drawn from cross-sectional designs, which poses limitations in determining causality.

Trends in fruit and vegetable consumption and dietary guidelines

Accumulating epidemiological evidence suggests that higher intakes of fruit and vegetables are associated with a decreased likelihood of non-communicable diseases (153-155) and depression.(141, 142) The WHO and Food Agriculture of the United Nations report have recommended daily consumption of fruit and vegetables with a minimum of 400g for the prevention of diet-related chronic diseases.(156)

However, the current average global fruit and vegetable consumption remains below the recommended daily consumption.(157, 158) A study by Frank et al.(159) confirmed that the overall prevalence of meeting the WHO recommendation for combined fruit and vegetable consumption was only 18% of 193,606 participants aged 15 years and over in 28 Low-Middle Income Countries. At the individual level by geographical region, the prevalence remained well below recommendations, with an estimation of 4.6% in low-income countries, 11.2% in lower-middle-income countries, and 27.2% in upper-middle-income countries.(159) It was estimated that the average daily intake of fruit and vegetable intake was only 1.15 servings and 2.46 servings, respectively.(159)

In Australia, the minimum recommended daily intake for adults is two servings of fruits (150g/serving) and five servings of vegetables (75g/serving).(160) The 2017-18 National Health Survey found that generally Australian adults aged 18 and above had modest daily intakes of fruit (1.7 servings) and low daily intakes of vegetables (2.4 servings).(161) The lowest daily intake of fruit and vegetable was observed among young adults aged 25-34, with 1.6 and 2.3 servings, respectively.(161) Overall, it was estimated that only 5.4% of Australian adults met the minimum daily servings of fruit and vegetables in 2017-18.(161)

book rationale

Depression remains a major public health concern, which significantly impacts the affected individuals, their families, and the community.(1-4) The screening phase is crucial to provide adequate treatment for affected individuals, yet some barriers hinder young adults from seeking help from mental health professionals. Despite improved health care access and treatments for depression, the proportion of people with depressive disorder receiving minimally adequate treatment is low.(107) With high prevalence rates and limitations of treatments, there is an urgent need for developing effective and affordable preventive strategies for depression.

Accumulating evidence suggests that healthy diets, particularly higher fruit and vegetables can be a promising intervention to reduce the likelihood of depression symptoms.(140-142, 151, 152) Therefore, there is an indication that the association between a healthy diet and lower depression symptoms may be driven by fruit and vegetables. However, previous studies focusing on the association between fruit and vegetable consumption and depression symptoms show mixed results. To date, the majority of the studies have been focused on older adults. Although young adulthood has been characterised as a period of crucial life transitions that may disrupt diet and influence mental health,(81, 82) limited studies have investigated this association.

To date, there is no systematic review evaluating the association between fruit and vegetable consumption and depression in young people and adults, focusing on findings from longitudinal cohort studies. Also, very few long-term prospective studies examine the effects of fruit and vegetable consumption and depression symptoms in young people and adults using population-based cohorts. Several prospective studies focusing on women indicate a potential role of fruit and vegetables in relation to depression.(148, 149) With higher incidence and lifetime prevalence in women, the second study is focused on young women populations to provide further evidence. In the current book, depression symptoms are the outcome of interest based on the screening for depression with validated and reliable instruments. In other words, depression in this book is not limited to clinical depression because a large number of depression cases are undiagnosed and untreated by mental health professionals. Therefore, this book project sought to investigate the potential role of fruit and vegetables to reduce the risk of depression symptoms.

book objectives

1. To evaluate and critically appraise the evidence on the association between fruit and vegetable intake and depressive symptoms in young people and adults aged 15–45 using longitudinal cohort studies.
2. To examine the differential effects of fruit and vegetables in relation to depression symptoms over a 15-year follow up period in the 1973-78 cohort of the Australian Longitudinal Study on Women's Health (ALSWH).

book overview

Figure 3 below depicts the link between book chapters. It begins from Chapter 1, which is the introduction. Chapter 2 presents Paper I, which is a systematic review. Chapter 3 presents the results from a secondary analysis from the 1973-78 cohort of the ALSWH (Paper II). Finally, Chapter 4 consists of a discussion and conclusion of the book, which summarises the findings from both studies, discusses the contribution of the current studies and provides key recommendations and future directions.

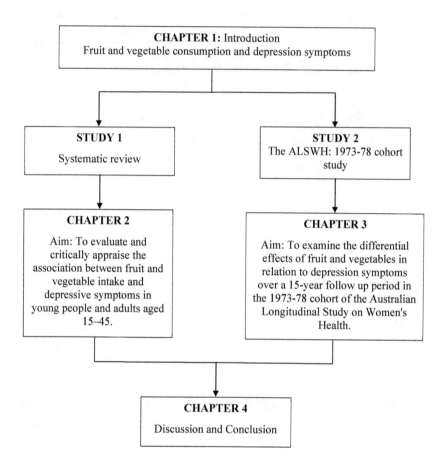

Figure 3. Overview of the studies undertaken in this Master's book.

References

1. Liu Q, He H, Yang J, Feng X, Zhao F, Lyu J. Changes in the global burden of depression from 1990 to 2017: Findings from the Global Burden of Disease study. J Psychiatr Res. 2020;126:134-40.
2. Lim GY, Tam WW, Lu Y, Ho CS, Zhang MW, Ho RC. Prevalence of Depression in the Community from 30 Countries between 1994 and 2014. Sci. 2018;8(1):2861.
3. Kessler RC, Bromet EJ. The epidemiology of depression across cultures. Annu Rev Public Health. 2013;34:119-38.
4. James SL, Abate D, Abate KH, Abay SM, Abbafati C, Abbasi N, et al. Global, regional, and national incidence, prevalence, and years lived with disability for 354 diseases and injuries for 195 countries and territories, 1990–2017: a systematic analysis for the Global Burden of Disease Study 2017. The Lancet. 2018;392(10159):1789-858.
5. Burcusa SL, Iacono WG. Risk for recurrence in depression. Clin Psychol Rev. 2007;27(8):959-85.
6. Vos T, Lim SS, Abbafati C, Abbas KM, Abbasi M, Abbasifard M, et al. Global burden of 369 diseases and injuries in 204 countries and territories, 1990–2019: a systematic analysis for the Global Burden of Disease Study 2019. The Lancet. 2020;396(10258):1204-22.
7. Roehrig C. Mental disorders top the list of the most costly conditions in the United States: $201 billion. Health Affair. 2016;35(6):1130-5.
8. Australian Institute of Health and Welfare. Mental health services in Australia [Internet]. Canberra: AIHW; 2021 [updated 2021 January 29, cited 2021 May 20]. Available from: https://www.aihw.gov.au/reports/mental-health-services/mental-health-services-in-australia/report-contents/expenditure-on-mental-health-related-services.
9. Jesulola E, Micalos P, Baguley IJ. Understanding the pathophysiology of depression: From monoamines to the neurogenesis hypothesis model - are we there yet? Behavioural Brain Research. 2018;341:79-90.
10. Weinberger AH, Gbedemah M, Martinez AM, Nash D, Galea S, Goodwin RD. Trends in depression prevalence in the USA from 2005 to 2015: widening disparities in vulnerable groups. Psychol Med. 2018;48(8):1308-15.
11. Babajide A, Ortin A, Wei C, Mufson L, Duarte CS. Transition cliffs for young adults with anxiety and depression: Is integrated mental health care a solution? The Journal of Behavioral Health Services & Research. 2020;47(2):275-92.
12. McLaughlin KA. The public health impact of major depression: a call for interdisciplinary prevention efforts. Prevention Science. 2011;12(4):361-71.
13. National Collaborating Centre for Mental Health (UK). Common mental health disorders: identification and pathways to care. Leicester (UK): British Psychological Society; 2011.
14. American Psychiatric Association. Diagnostic and statistical manual of mental disorders DSM-5. 5th ed. Washington, D.C: American Psychiatric Association; 2013.
15. Kerr LK, Kerr LD, Jr. Screening tools for depression in primary care: the effects of culture, gender, and somatic symptoms on the detection of depression. West J Med. 2001;175(5):349-52.
16. Beck AT, Ward CH, Mendelson M, Mock J, Erbaugh J. An inventory for measuring depression. Archives of General Psychiatry. 1961;4(6):561-71.
17. Radloff LS. The CES-D scale: A Self-report depression scale for research in the general population. Applied Psychological Measurement. 1977;1(3):385-401.
18. Kroenke K, Spitzer RL, Williams JBW. The PHQ-9. J Gen Intern Med. 2001;16(9):606-13.
19. Hamilton M. A rating scale for depression. J Neurol Neurosurg Psychiatry. 1960 Feb;23(1):56-62.

20. World Health Organization. Depression and other common mental disorders: global health estimates. Geneva: World Health Organization; 2017. Licence: CC BY-NC-SA 3.0 IGO. Available from: http://apps.who.int/iris/bitstream/10665/254610/1/WHO-MSD-MER-2017.2-eng.pdf?ua=1.
21. Gander F, Proyer RT, Ruch W, Wyss T. Strength-based positive interventions: further evidence for their potential in enhancing well-being and alleviating depression. Journal of Happiness Studies. 2013;14(4):1241-59.
22. Wood AM, Joseph S. The absence of positive psychological (eudemonic) well-being as a risk factor for depression: a ten year cohort study. J Affect Disord. 2010;122(3):213-7.
23. Lagnado AM, Gilchrist K, Smastuen MC, Memon A. Is subjective wellbeing associated with depression? A cross-sectional survey in Southeast England: Anjum Memon. European Journal of Public Health. 2017;27(suppl_3).
24. Grant F, Guille C, Sen S. Well-being and the risk of depression under stress. PLoS ONE. 2013;8(7):e67395-e.
25. Diener E, Suh EM, Lucas RE, Smith HL. Subjective well-being: three decades of progress. Psychol Bull. 1999;125(2):276-302.
26. Diener E. Subjective Well-Being: The Science of Happiness and a Proposal for a National Index. The American psychologist. 2000;55(1):34-43.
27. Proctor C. Subjective Well-Being (SWB). In: Michalos AC, editor. Encyclopedia of Quality of Life and Well-Being Research. Dordrecht: Springer Netherlands; 2014. p. 6437-41.
28. World Health Assembly. Global burden of mental disorders and the need for a comprehensive, coordinated response from health and social sectors at the country level: report by the Secretariat. Geneva: World Health Organization; 2012. Available from: https://apps.who.int/iris/handle/10665/78898
29. Kim GE, Jo MW, Shin YW. Increased prevalence of depression in South Korea from 2002 to 2013. Sci. 2020;10(1):16979.
30. Steffen A, Thom J, Jacobi F, Holstiege J, Bätzing J. Trends in prevalence of depression in Germany between 2009 and 2017 based on nationwide ambulatory claims data. J Affect Disord. 2020;271:239-47.
31. Noorbala AA, Bagheri Yazdi SA, Faghihzadeh S, Kamali K, Faghihzadeh E, Hajebi A, et al. Trends of mental health status in iranian population aged 15 and above between 1999 and 2015. Arch Iran Med. 2017;20(11 Suppl. 1):S2-S6.
32. Hidaka BH. Depression as a disease of modernity: explanations for increasing prevalence. J Affect Disord. 2012;140(3):205-14.
33. Moreno-Agostino D, Wu YT, Daskalopoulou C, Hasan MT, Huisman M, Prina M. Global trends in the prevalence and incidence of depression:a systematic review and meta-analysis. J Affect Disord. 2021;281:235-43.
34. Sloan DM, Sandt AR. Gender differences in depression. Women's Health. 2006;2(3):425-34.
35. Kuehner C. Why is depression more common among women than among men? The Lancet Psychiatry. 2017;4(2):146-58.
36. Picco L, Subramaniam M, Abdin E, Vaingankar JA, Chong SA. Gender differences in major depressive disorder: findings from the Singapore Mental Health Study. Singapore Med J. 2017;58(11):649-55.
37. Schuch JJJ, Roest AM, Nolen WA, Penninx BWJH, de Jonge P. Gender differences in major depressive disorder: results from the Netherlands study of depression and anxiety. J Affect Disord. 2014;156:156-63.
38. Salk RH, Hyde JS, Abramson LY. Gender differences in depression in representative national samples: meta-analyses of diagnoses and symptoms. Psychol Bull. 2017;143(8):783-822.

39. Eid RS, Gobinath AR, Galea LAM. Sex differences in depression: insights from clinical and preclinical studies. Progress in Neurobiology. 2019;176:86-102.
40. Labaka A, Goñi-Balentziaga O, Lebeña A, Pérez-Tejada J. Biological sex differences in depression: a systematic review. Biol Res Nurs. 2018;20(4):383-92.
41. Parker G, Brotchie H. Gender differences in depression. International Review of Psychiatry. 2010;22(5):429-36.
42. Falicov CJ. Culture, society and gender in depression. Journal of Family Therapy. 2003;25(4):371-87.
43. Shih JH, Eberhart NK, Hammen CL, Brennan PA. Differential exposure and reactivity to interpersonal stress predict sex differences in adolescent depression. J Clin Child Adolesc Psychol. 2006;35(1):103-15.
44. Fleisher WP, Katz LY. Early onset major depressive disorder. Paediatr Child Health. 2001;6(7):444-8.
45. Klein DN, Glenn CR, Kosty DB, Seeley JR, Rohde P, Lewinsohn PM. Predictors of first lifetime onset of major depressive disorder in young adulthood. J Abnorm Psychol. 2013;122(1):1-6.
46. Copeland W, Shanahan L, Costello EJ, Angold A. Cumulative prevalence of psychiatric disorders by young adulthood: a prospective cohort analysis from the Great Smoky Mountains Study. Journal of the American Academy of Child and Adolescent Psychiatry. 2011;50(3):252-61.
47. Gustavson K, Knudsen AK, Nesvåg R, Knudsen GP, Vollset SE, Reichborn-Kjennerud T. Prevalence and stability of mental disorders among young adults: findings from a longitudinal study. BMC Psychiatry. 2018;18(1):65.
48. National Institute of Mental Health (US). Major depression [Internet]. Maryland (US): National Institute of Mental Health; 2019 [updated 2019 February, cited 2021 March 3]. Available from: https://www.nimh.nih.gov/health/statistics/major-depression.
49. Goldney RD, Eckert KA, Hawthorne G, Taylor AW. Changes in the prevalence of major depression in an Australian community sample between 1998 and 2008. Australian & New Zealand Journal of Psychiatry. 2010;44(10):901-10.
50. Australian Bureau of Statistics. National health survey: first results [Internet]. Canberra: Australian Bureau of Statistics; 2018 [updated 2018 December 12, cited 2021 March 3]. Available from: https://www.abs.gov.au/statistics/health/health-conditions-and-risks/national-health-survey-first-results/latest-release.
51. Australian Institute of Health and Welfare. Burden of disease [Internet]. Canberra: Australian Institute of Health and Welfare; 2020 [updated 2021 February 18, cited 2021 March 3]. Available from: https://www.aihw.gov.au/reports/australias-health/burden-of-disease.
52. Australian Government Productivity Commision. Mental health: productivity commission inquiry report. Canberra: Australian Government Productivity Commision; 30 June 2020. 83 p. Report No: 95. Available from: https://www.pc.gov.au/inquiries/completed/mental-health/report/mental-health-volume1.pdf.
53. Trautmann S, Rehm J, Wittchen H-U. The economic costs of mental disorders: do our societies react appropriately to the burden of mental disorders? EMBO Rep. 2016;17(9):1245-9.
54. The Lancet Global Health. Mental health matters. The Lancet Global Health. 2020;8(11):e1352.
55. Malik MA, Khan MM. Economic burden of mental illnesses in Pakistan. J Ment Health Policy Econ. 2016;19(3):155-66.

56. Hu TW, He Y, Zhang M, Chen N. Economic costs of depression in China. Soc Psychiatry Psychiatr Epidemiol. 2007;42(2):110-6.
57. Shadrina M, Bondarenko EA, Slominsky PA. Genetics factors in major depression disease. Frontiers in psychiatry. 2018;9:334-.
58. National Research Council (US) and Institute of Medicine (US) Committee on Depression PP, and the Healthy Development of Children. Depression in parents, parenting, and children: opportunities to improve identification, treatment, and prevention. Washington (DC): National Academies Press (US); 2009. Available from: https://www.ncbi.nlm.nih.gov/books/NBK215119/.
59. Sullivan PF, Neale MC, Kendler KS. Genetic epidemiology of major depression: review and meta-analysis. Am J Psychiatry. 2000;157(10):1552-62.
60. Kendler KS, Gatz M, Gardner CO, Pedersen NL. A Swedish national twin study of lifetime major depression. Am J Psychiatry. 2006;163(1):109-14.
61. Shao X, Zhu G. Associations among monoamine neurotransmitter pathways, personality traits, and major depressive disorder. Frontiers in psychiatry. 2020;11:381-.
62. Pan JX, Xia JJ, Deng FL, Liang WW, Wu J, Yin BM, et al. Diagnosis of major depressive disorder based on changes in multiple plasma neurotransmitters: a targeted metabolomics study. Transl Psychiatry. 2018;8(1):130.
63. Dean J, Keshavan M. The neurobiology of depression: an integrated view. Asian Journal of Psychiatry. 2017;27:101-11.
64. Kaltenboeck A, Harmer C. The neuroscience of depressive disorders: a brief review of the past and some considerations about the future. Brain and Neuroscience Advances. 2018;2:2398212818799269.
65. Hasler G. Pathophysiology of depression: do we have any solid evidence of interest to clinicians? World Psychiatry. 2010;9(3):155-61.
66. Brigitta B. Pathophysiology of depression and mechanisms of treatment. Dialogues Clin Neurosci. 2002;4(1):7-20.
67. Verduijn J, Milaneschi Y, Schoevers RA, van Hemert AM, Beekman ATF, Penninx BWJH. Pathophysiology of major depressive disorder: mechanisms involved in etiology are not associated with clinical progression. Translational Psychiatry. 2015;5(9):e649-e.
68. Maletic V, Eramo A, Gwin K, Offord SJ, Duffy RA. The role of norepinephrine and its α-adrenergic receptors in the pathophysiology and treatment of major depressive disorder and schizophrenia: a systematic Review. Frontiers in psychiatry. 2017;8:42-.
69. Grace AA. Dysregulation of the dopamine system in the pathophysiology of schizophrenia and depression. Nature Reviews Neuroscience. 2016;17(8):524-32.
70. Tiet QQ, Bird HR, Hoven CW, Moore R, Wu P, Wicks J, et al. Relationship between specific adverse life events and psychiatric disorders. Journal of Abnormal Child Psychology. 2001;29(2):153-64.
71. Francis LE, Kypriotakis G, O'Toole EE, Bowman KF, Rose JH. Grief and risk of depression in context: the emotional outcomes of bereaved cancer caregivers. Journal of Death and Dying. 2015;70(4):351-79.
72. Luecken LJ. Attachment and loss experiences during childhood are associated with adult hostility, depression, and social support. J Psychosom Res. 2000;49(1):85-91.
73. Ali F, Mostafa F, Hosein A, Elham Davtalab E, Mohammad M, Vahab Asl R, et al. Early marriage and negative life events affect on depression in young adults and adolescents. Arch Iran Med. 2020;23(2):90.
74. Nishikawa S, Fujisawa TX, Kojima M, Tomoda A. Type and timing of negative life events are associated with adolescent depression. Frontiers in psychiatry. 2018;9:41-.

75. Patton GC, Coffey C, Posterino M, Carlin JB, Bowes G. Life events and early onset depression: cause or consequence? Psychol Med. 2003;33(7):1203-10.
76. Stikkelbroek Y, Bodden DHM, Kleinjan M, Reijnders M, van Baar AL. Adolescent depression and negative life events, the mediating role of cognitive emotion regulation. PLoS ONE. 2016;11(8):e0161062-e.
77. Negele A, Kaufhold J, Kallenbach L, Leuzinger-Bohleber M. Childhood trauma and its relation to chronic depression in adulthood. Depress Res Treat. 2015;2015:650804-.
78. Mandelli L, Petrelli C, Serretti A. The role of specific early trauma in adult depression: a meta-analysis of published literature. Childhood trauma and adult depression. European Psychiatry. 2015;30(6):665-80.
79. Wei J, Gong Y, Wang X, Shi J, Ding H, Zhang M, et al. Gender differences in the relationships between different types of childhood trauma and resilience on depressive symptoms among Chinese adolescents. Prev Med. 2021;148:106523.
80. Gallo EAG, Munhoz TN, Loret de Mola C, Murray J. Gender differences in the effects of childhood maltreatment on adult depression and anxiety: a systematic review and meta-analysis. Child Abuse Negl. 2018;79(1873-7757):107-14.
81. Arnett JJ, Žukauskienė R, Sugimura K. The new life stage of emerging adulthood at ages 18–29 years: implications for mental health. The Lancet Psychiatry. 2014;1(7):569-76.
82. Arnett JJ. Emerging adulthood: a theory of development from the late teens through the twenties. American Psychological Association. 2000;55(5):469-80.
83. Edgerton JD, Shaw S, Roberts LW. An exploration of depression symptom trajectories, and their predictors, in a Canadian sample of emerging adults. Emerging Adulthood. 2018;7(5):352-62.
84. Sarris J, Thomson R, Hargraves F, Eaton M, de Manincor M, Veronese N, et al. Multiple lifestyle factors and depressed mood: a cross-sectional and longitudinal analysis of the UK Biobank (N = 84,860). BMC Med. 2020;18(1):354.
85. Schweren LJS, Larsson H, Vinke PC, Li L, Kvalvik LG, Arias-Vasquez A, et al. Diet quality, stress and common mental health problems: a cohort study of 121,008 adults. Clin Nutr. 2021;40(3):901-6.
86. Sánchez-Villegas A, Toledo E, de Irala J, Ruiz-Canela M, Pla-Vidal J, Martínez-González MA. Fast-food and commercial baked goods consumption and the risk of depression. Public Health Nutr. 2012;15(3):424-32.
87. Cabello M, Miret M, Caballero FF, Chatterji S, Naidoo N, Kowal P, et al. The role of unhealthy lifestyles in the incidence and persistence of depression: a longitudinal general population study in four emerging countries. Global Health. 2017;13(1):18-.
88. Bélair M-A, Kohen DE, Kingsbury M, Colman I. Relationship between leisure time physical activity, sedentary behaviour and symptoms of depression and anxiety: evidence from a population-based sample of Canadian adolescents. BMJ Open. 2018;8(10):e021119.
89. Roberts RE, Duong HT. The prospective association between sleep deprivation and depression among adolescents. Sleep. 2014;37(2):239-44.
90. Lopresti AL, Hood SD, Drummond PD. A review of lifestyle factors that contribute to important pathways associated with major depression: diet, sleep and exercise. J Affect Disord. 2013;148(1):12-27.
91. Boden JM, Fergusson DM. Alcohol and depression. Addiction. 2011;106(5):906-14.
92. Ning K, Gondek D, Patalay P, Ploubidis GB. The association between early life mental health and alcohol use behaviours in adulthood: a systematic review. PLoS ONE. 2020;15(2):e0228667.

93. Ranjit A, Buchwald J, Latvala A, Heikkilä K, Tuulio-Henriksson A, Rose RJ, et al. Predictive association of smoking with depressive symptoms: a longitudinal study of adolescent twins. Prevention Science. 2019;20(7):1021-30.
94. Fluharty M, Taylor AE, Grabski M, Munafò MR. The association of cigarette smoking with depression and anxiety: a systematic review. Nicotine Tob Res. 2017;19(1):3-13.
95. Furihata R, Konno C, Suzuki M, Takahashi S, Kaneita Y, Ohida T, et al. Unhealthy lifestyle factors and depressive symptoms: a Japanese general adult population survey. J Affect Disord. 2018;234:156-61.
96. Levola J, Pitkanen T, Kampman O, Aalto M. The association of alcohol use and quality of life in depressed and non-depressed individuals: a cross-sectional general population study. Qual Life Res. 2018;27(5):1217-26.
97. Jacka FN, Cherbuin N, Anstey KJ, Butterworth P. Dietary patterns and depressive symptoms over time: examining the relationships with socioeconomic position, health behaviours and cardiovascular risk. PLoS ONE. 2014;9(1):e87657.
98. Cuijpers P, Pineda BS, Quero S, Karyotaki E, Struijs SY, Figueroa CA, et al. Psychological interventions to prevent the onset of depressive disorders: a meta-analysis of randomized controlled trials. Clin Psychol Rev. 2021;83:101955.
99. Cipriani A, Furukawa TA, Salanti G, Chaimani A, Atkinson LZ, Ogawa Y, et al. Comparative efficacy and acceptability of 21 antidepressant drugs for the acute treatment of adults with major depressive disorder: a systematic review and network meta-analysis. The Lancet. 2018;391(10128):1357-66.
100. Lakhan SE, Vieira KF. Nutritional therapies for mental disorders. Nutr J. 2008;7:2-.
101. Hengartner MP. How effective are antidepressants for depression over the long term? A critical review of relapse prevention trials and the issue of withdrawal confounding. Therapeutic Advances in Psychopharmacology. 2020;10:2045125320921694.
102. Kendrick T. Long-term antidepressant treatment: time for a review? Prescriber. 2015;26(19):7-10.
103. Gautam M, Tripathi A, Deshmukh D, Gaur M. Cognitive behavioral therapy for depression. Indian Journal of Psychiatry. 2020;62(Suppl 2):S223-S9.
104. Cuijpers P, Quero S, Dowrick C, Arroll B. Psychological treatment of depression in primary care: recent developments. Current Psychiatry Reports. 2019;21(12):129.
105. Kolovos S, Kleiboer A, Cuijpers P. Effect of psychotherapy for depression on quality of life: meta-analysis. British Journal of Psychiatry. 2016;209(6):460-8.
106. Chisholm D, Sweeny K, Sheehan P, Rasmussen B, Smit F, Cuijpers P, et al. Scaling-up treatment of depression and anxiety: a global return on investment analysis. The Lancet Psychiatry. 2016;3(5):415-24.
107. Thornicroft G, Chatterji S, Evans-Lacko S, Gruber M, Sampson N, Aguilar-Gaxiola S, et al. Undertreatment of people with major depressive disorder in 21 countries. British Journal of Psychiatry. 2017;210(2):119-24.
108. van Zoonen K, Buntrock C, Ebert DD, Smit F, Reynolds CF, III, Beekman ATF, et al. Preventing the onset of major depressive disorder: a meta-analytic review of psychological interventions. Int J Epidemiol. 2014;43(2):318-29.
109. Andrews G, Szabo M, Burns J. Preventing major depression in young people. British Journal of Psychiatry. 2002;181(6):460-2.
110. Cuijpers P, van Straten A, Smit F, Mihalopoulos C, Beekman A. Preventing the onset of depressive disorders: a meta-analytic review of psychological interventions. Am J Psychiatry. 2008;165(10):1272-80.

111. Firth J, Solmi M, Wootton RE, Vancampfort D, Schuch FB, Hoare E, et al. A meta-review of "lifestyle psychiatry": the role of exercise, smoking, diet and sleep in the prevention and treatment of mental disorders. World Psychiatry. 2020;19(3):360-80.
112. van Dammen L, Wekker V, de Rooij SR, Groen H, Hoek A, Roseboom TJ. A systematic review and meta-analysis of lifestyle interventions in women of reproductive age with overweight or obesity: the effects on symptoms of depression and anxiety. Obes Rev. 2018;19(12):1679-87.
113. Hu MX, Turner D, Generaal E, Bos D, Ikram MK, Ikram MA, et al. Exercise interventions for the prevention of depression: a systematic review of meta-analyses. BMC Public Health. 2020;20(1):1255.
114. Josefsson T, Lindwall M, Archer T. Physical exercise intervention in depressive disorders: meta-analysis and systematic review. Scand J Med Sci Sports. 2014;24(2):259-72.
115. Ljungberg T, Bondza E, Lethin C. Evidence of the importance of dietary habits regarding depressive symptoms and depression. Int J Environ Res Public Health. 2020;17(5):1616.
116. Rooney C, McKinley MC, Woodside JV. A systematic review of the potential role of fruit and vegetables in depression. Proc Nutr Soc. 2016;75(OCE3):E162.
117. Rooney C, McKinley MC, Woodside JV. The potential role of fruit and vegetables in aspects of psychological well-being: a review of the literature and future directions. Proc Nutr Soc. 2013;72(4):420-32.
118. Tuso PJ, Ismail MH, Ha BP, Bartolotto C. Nutritional update for physicians: plant-based diets. Perm J. 2013;17(2):61-6.
119. Francis HM, Stevenson RJ. Potential for diet to prevent and remediate cognitive deficits in neurological disorders. Nutrition Reviews. 2018;76(3):204-17.
120. Null G, Pennesi L, Feldman M. Nutrition and lifestyle intervention on mood and neurological disorders. Journal of Evidence-Based Complementary & Alternative Medicine. 2016;22(1):68-74.
121. Lassale C, Batty GD, Baghdadli A, Jacka F, Sanchez-Villegas A, Kivimaki M, et al. Healthy dietary indices and risk of depressive outcomes: a systematic review and meta-analysis of observational studies. Mol Psychiatry. 2019;24(7):965-86.
122. Altun A, Brown H, Szoeke C, Goodwill AM. The Mediterranean dietary pattern and depression risk: a systematic review. Neurology, Psychiatry and Brain Research. 2019;33:1-10.
123. Lai JS, Hiles S, Bisquera A, Hure AJ, McEvoy M, Attia J. A systematic review and meta-analysis of dietary patterns and depression in community-dwelling adults. Am J Clin Nutr. 2014;99(1):181-97.
124. Chopra C, Mandalika S, Kinger N. Does diet play a role in the prevention and management of depression among adolescents? A narrative review. Nutrition and Health. 2021;27(2):243-63.
125. Francis HM, Stevenson RJ, Chambers JR, Gupta D, Newey B, Lim CK. A brief diet intervention can reduce symptoms of depression in young adults – a randomised controlled trial. PLoS ONE. 2019;14(10):e0222768.
126. Firth J, Marx W, Dash S, Carney R, Teasdale SB, Solmi M, et al. The effects of dietary improvement on symptoms of depression and anxiety: a meta-analysis of randomized controlled trials. Psychosom Med. 2019;81(3).
127. Reynolds E. Vitamin B12, folic acid, and the nervous system. The Lancet Neurology. 2006;5(11):949-60.
128. Kirkland AE, Sarlo GL, Holton KF. The role of magnesium in neurological disorders. Nutrients. 2018;10(6):730.

129. Afshin A, Sur PJ, Ferrara G, Salama JS, Mullany EC, Abate KH, et al. Health effects of dietary risks in 195 countries, 1990–2017: A systematic analysis for the Global Burden of Disease Study 2017. The Lancet (British edition). 2019;393(10184):1958–72.
130. Aune D, Giovannucci E, Boffetta P, Fadnes LT, Keum N, Norat T, et al. Fruit and vegetable intake and the risk of cardiovascular disease, total cancer and all-cause mortality-a systematic review and dose-response meta-analysis of prospective studies. Int J Epidemiol. 2017;46(3):1029-56.
131. Rissanen TH, Voutilainen S, Virtanen JK, Venho B, Vanharanta M, Mursu J, et al. Low intake of fruits, berries and vegetables is associated with excess mortality in men: the Kuopio Ischaemic Heart Disease Risk Factor (KIHD) Study. Journal of Nutrition. 2003;133(1):199-204.
132. Key TJ. Fruit and vegetables and cancer risk. Br J Cancer. 2011;104(1):6-11.
133. Arnotti K, Bamber M. Fruit and vegetable consumption in overweight or obese individuals: a meta-analysis. Western Journal of Nursing Research. 2019;42(4):306-14.
134. Dehghan M, Akhtar-Danesh N, Merchant AT. Factors associated with fruit and vegetable consumption among adults. Journal of Human Nutrition and Dietetics. 2011;24(2):128-34.
135. Ju SY, Park YK. Low fruit and vegetable intake is associated with depression among Korean adults in data from the 2014 Korea National Health and Nutrition Examination Survey. J Health Popul Nutr. 2019;38(1):39.
136. Liu MW, Chen QT, Towne SD, Jr., Zhang J, Yu HJ, Tang R, et al. Fruit and vegetable intake in relation to depressive and anxiety symptoms among adolescents in 25 low- and middle-income countries. J Affect Disord. 2020;261:172-80.
137. Branca F, Lartey A, Oenema S, Aguayo V, Stordalen GA, Richardson R, et al. Transforming the food system to fight non-communicable diseases. BMJ. 2019;364:l296.
138. McMartin SE, Jacka FN, Colman I. The association between fruit and vegetable consumption and mental health disorders: evidence from five waves of a national survey of Canadians. Prev Med. 2013;56(3-4):225-30.
139. Slavin JL, Lloyd B. Health benefits of fruits and vegetables. Advances in Nutrition. 2012;3(4):506-16.
140. Conner TS, Brookie KL, Carr AC, Mainvil LA, Vissers MCM. Let them eat fruit! The effect of fruit and vegetable consumption on psychological well-being in young adults: a randomized controlled trial. PLoS ONE. 2017;12(2):e0171206-e.
141. Saghafian F, Malmir H, Saneei P, Milajerdi A, Larijani B, Esmaillzadeh A. Fruit and vegetable consumption and risk of depression: accumulative evidence from an updated systematic review and meta-analysis of epidemiological studies. Br J Nutr. 2018;119(10):1087-101.
142. Liu X, Yan Y, Li F, Zhang D. Fruit and vegetable consumption and the risk of depression: A meta-analysis. Nutrition. 2016;32(3):296-302.
143. Saghafian F, Malmir H, Saneei P, Keshteli AH, Hosseinzadeh-Attar MJ, Afshar H, et al. Consumption of fruit and vegetables in relation with psychological disorders in Iranian adults. Eur J Nutr. 2018;57(6):2295-306.
144. Pengpid S, Peltzer K. Association between fruit/vegetable consumption and mental-health-related quality of life, major depression, and generalized anxiety disorder: a longitudinal study in Thailand. Iran J Psychiatr Behav Sci. 2019;13(2).
145. Wu S, Fisher-Hoch SP, Reininger BM, McCormick JB. Association between fruit and vegetable intake and symptoms of mental health conditions in Mexican Americans. Health Psychol. 2018;37(11):1059-66.

146. Bhattacharyya M, Marston L, Walters K, D'Costa G, King M, Nazareth I. Psychological distress, gender and dietary factors in South Asians: a cross-sectional survey. Public Health Nutr. 2014;17(7):1538-46.
147. Kim TH, Choi JY, Lee HH, Park Y. Associations between dietary pattern and depression in Korean adolescent girls. J Pediatr Adolesc Gynecol. 2015;28(6):533-7.
148. Mihrshahi S, Dobson AJ, Mishra GD. Fruit and vegetable consumption and prevalence and incidence of depressive symptoms in mid-age women: results from the Australian Longitudinal Study On Women's Health. Eur J Clin Nutr. 2015;69(5):585-91.
149. Chang SC, Cassidy A, Willett WC, Rimm EB, O'Reilly EJ, Okereke OI. Dietary flavonoid intake and risk of incident depression in midlife and older women. Am J Clin Nutr. 2016;104(3):704-14.
150. Huang Q, Liu H, Suzuki K, Ma S, Liu C. Linking what we eat to our mood: a review of diet, dietary antioxidants, and depression. Antioxidants. 2019;8(9):376.
151. Angelino D, Godos J, Ghelfi F, Tieri M, Titta L, Lafranconi A, et al. Fruit and vegetable consumption and health outcomes: an umbrella review of observational studies. Int J Food Sci Nutr. 2019;70(6):652-67.
152. Głąbska D, Guzek D, Groele B, Gutkowska K. Fruit and vegetable intake and mental health in adults: a systematic review. Nutrients. 2020;12(1):115.
153. Wang X, Ouyang Y, Liu J, Zhu M, Zhao G, Bao W, et al. Fruit and vegetable consumption and mortality from all causes, cardiovascular disease, and cancer: systematic review and dose-response meta-analysis of prospective cohort studies. BMJ. 2014;349:g4490.
154. Aune D, Giovannucci E, Boffetta P, Fadnes LT, Keum N, Norat T, et al. Fruit and vegetable intake and the risk of cardiovascular disease, total cancer and all-cause mortality-a systematic review and dose-response meta-analysis of prospective studies. Int J Epidemiol. 2017;46(3):1029-56.
155. Yip CSC, Chan W, Fielding R. The associations of fruit and vegetable intakes with burden of diseases: a systematic review of meta-analyses. J Acad Nutri Diet. 2019;119(3):464-81.
156. World Health Organization and Food and Agriculture Organization of the United Nations. Fruit and vegetables for health: report of the Joint FAO/WHO Workshop on Fruit and Vegetables for Health, 1-3 September 2004, Kobe, Japan. Geneva: World Health Organization and Food and Agriculture Organization of the United Nations; 2005. 46 p. Available from: https://apps.who.int/iris/handle/10665/43143.
157. Kalmpourtzidou A, Eilander A, Talsma EF. Global vegetable intake and supply compared to recommendations: a systematic review. Nutrients. 2020;12(6):1558.
158. Mason-D'Croz D, Bogard JR, Sulser TB, Cenacchi N, Dunston S, Herrero M, et al. Gaps between fruit and vegetable production, demand, and recommended consumption at global and national levels: an integrated modelling study. The Lancet Planetary Health. 2019;3(7):e318-e29.
159. Frank SM, Webster J, McKenzie B, Geldsetzer P, Manne-Goehler J, Andall-Brereton G, et al. Consumption of fruits and vegetables among individuals 15 years and older in 28 low- and middle-income countries. J Nutr. 2019;149(7):1252-9.
160. World Health Organization and Food and Agriculture Organization of the United Nations. Fruit and vegetables for health: report of the Joint FAO/WHO Workshop on Fruit and Vegetables for Health, 1-3 September 2004, Kobe, Japan. Geneva: World Health Organization and Food and Agriculture Organization of the United Nations; 2005. 46 p. Available from: https://apps.who.int/iris/handle/10665/43143
161. Australian Bureau of Statistics. Dietary behaviour [Internet]. Canberra: Australian Bureau of Statistics; 2018 [updated 2018 December 12, cited 2021 April 3]. Available from:

https://www.abs.gov.au/statistics/health/health-conditions-and-risks/dietary-behaviour/latest-release#data-download.

Chapter 2:

Study 1: Association between fruit and vegetable consumption and depression symptoms in young people and adults aged 15-45: a systematic review of cohort studies

Rationale for the systematic review

Rapid increases in the prevalence of depression in young people and adults over recent years mean that it is necessary to develop preventive interventions urgently.(1-4) A growing body of research suggests that diet and lifestyle factors play an important role in the development of depression.(5-11) One notable part of a healthy diet, higher fruit and vegetable consumption, is associated with a reduced risk of depression.(12-14) As described in Chapter 1, some positive associations were observed between fruit and vegetable consumption and depression. However, a number of systematic reviews highlighted discordant findings.(15-18) Inherent bias may influence the results due to a large number of cross-sectional studies included.(19-21)

In order to obtain a clearer sequential relationship, the current systematic review aimed to evaluate the existing longitudinal literature for the association between fruit and vegetable consumption and depression symptoms in young people and adults aged 15-45. This age group was chosen because the current trends in depression indicate that young populations are particularly susceptible to suffer from this debilitating disorder.(1-4) Moreover, it is the age group with the highest prevalence in depression and suicide in Australia.(22)

This chapter includes the systematic review of the association between fruit and vegetable consumption and depression symptoms in young people and adults aged 15-45. The systematic review is published as:

Dharmayani PNA, Juergens M, Allman-Farinelli M, Mihrshahi S. Association between Fruit and Vegetable Consumption and Depression Symptoms in Young People and Adults Aged 15-45: A Systematic Review of Cohort Studies. International Journal of Environmental Research and Public Health. 2021;18(2):780–.

Article content

The article content is published under an open access Creative Common CC BY license. The original article can be accessed at the publisher's website: https://www.mdpi.com/1660-4601/18/2/780. The appendices presented in this article can be found in Appendix A of the book.

Author contributions: SM and MA-F conceptualised the study including the scope and preliminary search terms. PNAD and MJ identified and screened potentially relevant studies. PNAD, MJ, and SM screened and scrutinised full-text studies for eligibility. PNAD and MJ undertook data extraction, which was validated by SM and MA-F. PNAD and SM appraised the study quality and risk of bias. PNAD (90%) and MJ (10%) wrote the paper, then SM and MA-F reviewed and edited the paper. All the authors approved the final version of the manuscript.

Review

Association between Fruit and Vegetable Consumption and Depression Symptoms in Young People and Adults Aged 15–45: A Systematic Review of Cohort Studies

Putu Novi Arfirsta Dharmayani [1], Melissa Juergens [2], Margaret Allman-Farinelli [2,3] and Seema Mihrshahi [1,3,*]

1. Department of Health Systems and Populations, Faculty of Medicine, Health and Human Sciences, Macquarie University, Sydney, NSW 2109, Australia; putu-novi-arfirsta.dharmaya@hdr.mq.edu.au
2. Discipline of Nutrition and Dietetics, School of Life and Environmental Sciences, Faculty of Science, University of Sydney, Sydney, NSW 2006, Australia; mjue0385@uni.sydney.edu.au (M.J.); margaret.allman-farinelli@sydney.edu.au (M.A.-F.)
3. Prevention Research Collaboration, Sydney Medical School & Sydney School of Public Health, University of Sydney, Sydney, NSW 2006, Australia
* Correspondence: seema.mihrshahi@mq.edu.au; Tel.: +61-29850-2468

Citation: Dharmayani, P.N.A.; Juergens, M.; Allman-Farinelli, M.; Mihrshahi, S. Association between Fruit and Vegetable Consumption and Depression Symptoms in Young People and Adults Aged 15–45: A Systematic Review of Cohort Studies. *Int. J. Environ. Res. Public Health* **2021**, *18*, 780. https://doi.org/10.3390/ijerph18020780

Received: 14 December 2020
Accepted: 15 January 2021
Published: 18 January 2021

Publisher's Note: MDPI stays neutral with regard to jurisdictional claims in published maps and institutional affiliations.

Copyright: © 2021 by the authors. Licensee MDPI, Basel, Switzerland. This article is an open access article distributed under the terms and conditions of the Creative Commons Attribution (CC BY) license (https://creativecommons.org/licenses/by/4.0/).

Abstract: Higher consumption of fruit and vegetables has been associated with a lower risk of various chronic diseases including coronary heart disease, obesity, and certain cancers. Recently, fruit and vegetable intake has also been linked with mental health, including depression; however, this area is largely unexplored studies in young people and adults. This systematic review aimed to evaluate the association between fruit and vegetable intake and depressive symptoms in young people and adults aged 15–45. The review used a predefined protocol registered with International Prospective Register of Systematic Reviews (PROSPERO) database (ID no: CRD42018091642). The systematic review focused on peer-reviewed cohort studies published from 1 January 2000 to 31 August 2020 using searches of six electronic databases. The exposure was fruit and vegetable consumption analysed both separately and/or together, and the outcome was depression or depressive symptoms. Data from eligible studies were extracted according to predefined criteria and the studies were appraised using the Newcastle–Ottawa Scale (NOS) for cohort studies to evaluate for study quality and risk of bias. A total of 12 studies from seven countries were deemed eligible and included in the qualitative synthesis, one study was categorised as "very good" quality, nine studies were "good" quality, and two studies were "moderate" quality by the quality assessment based on the total score for the NOS. The majority of cohort studies support the evidence that fruit consumption is associated with decreased risk of developing depression. However, the inconsistent results were observed when the effects of vegetable consumption were analysed independently, and the effects of fruit and vegetables combined were analysed. Despite this, the evidence seems to be building that a possible association exists, and this may have implications for addressing the burden of mental illness in young people and adults aged 15–45 years. More well-designed prospective cohort studies are needed to provide more robust evidence on the relationship between fruit and vegetable intake and depression.

Keywords: fruit; vegetables; depressive symptoms; depression; young people; young adult; nutrition; diet

1. Introduction

Depression is a debilitating, chronic, and reoccurring condition that has become a major public health concern worldwide. In 2017 it was estimated that 300 million people, accounting for 4.4% of the global population, suffered from this disorder [1,2]. The number of incident cases of depression increased by almost 50% between 1990 and 2017 [3]. Major depressive disorder (MDD) is the second leading cause of years lived with disability and a large contributor to the global burden of disease globally [2], making it a substantial economic burden for countries. The peak age of onset of mental disorders, including depression, typically occurs during a period of life transition in early adulthood making it an important time for prevention strategies [4–6]. The percentage change in number of disability adjusted life years (DALYs) between 1990–2009 in depressive symptoms has risen dramatically in those aged 10–24 and aged 25–49, an increase of 20.7% and an increase of 53.2%, respectively [7]. Moreover, suicide is the second leading cause of death in young people aged 15–29 years in 2016 [8]. These alarming numbers emphasise the importance of preventing the onset on mental disorders as a priority for public health intervention.

The complex nature of the disease makes it difficult to attribute to a particular cause but depression has been linked to numerous biopsychosocial and lifestyle factors [9]. There has been growing interest recently in the plausible role of dietary factors as protective factors against depressive symptoms. Several systematic reviews of diet–depression studies have concluded that adhering to healthy dietary patterns is associated with reduced risk of depressive symptoms [10–13]. Particularly, higher fruit and vegetable consumption is widely recognized being important for improving mental health status [14–16]. However, the findings from previous studies on the association between the intake of fruit and vegetables and depression in young adults have tended to have contradictory conclusions. Some studies showed that higher intake of fruit and vegetables was associated with a lower likelihood of depressive symptoms [17–19], whereas other studies found no significant associations [20–22]. Recent systematic reviews indicated that an increase of fruits and vegetables intake may protect against the risk of depression and depressive symptoms in adults [23,24]. In older adult (>50 years) populations, many studies have shown associations between fruit and vegetable consumption and lower odds of depression development [25–27]. A recent systematic review in adolescents concluded that a potential of positive association between fruit and vegetable intake and mental health [28]. Contrarily, a 2016 systematic review conducted in children and young people aged 18 years and below observed that most studies found no significant association between fruit and vegetable consumption and mood [29].

The exact mechanisms by which fruits and vegetables are thought to lead to a decreased risk of depression are yet to be precisely identified. However, there are some evidence of an association with nutrients such as magnesium, zinc, and antioxidants such as vitamin C, E, and folate, found in these foods [30–35]. One possible pathway involves folate, a common vitamin found in foods such as leafy green vegetables, legumes, beans, and citrus fruits. Folate plays a critical role in the regeneration of tetrahydrobiopterin (BH4) and re-methylation of homocysteine which leads to the production of S-adenosylmethionine (SAMe) [33]. Moreover, both SAMe and BH4 are essential cofactors in the production of neurotransmitters such as serotonin, dopamine, and epinephrine, all which play a critical role in mood regulation. Several research studies exist linking folate deficiencies to depression [33,36–38].

Existing systematic literature reviews examining the diet–depression relationship tend to be inclusive of all study designs, and most of the included studies are cross-sectional studies [12,39–42]. This poses a methodological limitation when inferring causation in the context of diet-depression relationship [10]. Moreover, this limitation may contribute to inconsistent findings in previous systematic reviews [40]. Cohort studies have an advantage in that they are prospectively studying the associations between diet and depression and a clearer sequential relationship can be seen between exposure and outcome. Few studies have explored the relationship, especially in young people and adults aged 15–45. They remain a relatively neglected age group compared with children and older adults in diet-depression research, although the proportion of persons with depression in this age group is seen to dramatically increase [43,44] and healthy behaviour is more likely to decline during the transition to adulthood [45]. Moreover, a systematic review highlighted that emerging adulthood is a risk period for both low diet quality, including inadequate fruit and vegetable intake, and poor mental health [46]. In Australia, the 12 month prevalence of mental disorders in people aged

16–44 years was approximately 25% [47]. In this systematic review, we aimed to evaluate the association the between fruit and vegetables intake and depressive symptoms in young people and adults aged 15–45 using longitudinal cohort studies.

2. Materials and Methods

2.1. Study Design

The PRISMA framework was used to guide the reporting of methodology and outcomes [48]. The review used a predefined protocol registered with International Prospective Register of Systematic Reviews (PROSPERO) database (ID no: CRD42018091642) and can be accessed at: https://www.crd.york.ac.uk/PROSPERO/display_record.php?RecordID=91642.

2.2. Eligibility Criteria

The detailed inclusion and exclusion are shown in Supplementary Table S1. The following criteria was used—(1) studies in healthy individuals aged 15–45 years old. This age group was chosen because they are more likely to be a healthy population with less occurrence of chronic disease compared to mid-aged and older adult populations. During this period of life stage, key life transitions occur and their health behaviour, including diet, may change. (2) study design was restricted to original cohort studies with a follow up time of a year or longer. Due to the nature of depression, long-term follow up may well be desirable and appropriate to allow sufficient time to ascertain the occurrence of depression. Usually 12-month prevalence estimates are used to present the prevalence of mental disorders. (3) the exposure was fruit and vegetable intake analysed both separately and/or together; and (4) the outcome of studies was depression or depressive symptoms.

Studies were excluded if (1) they had study designs other than a longitudinal cohort; (2) they were published prior to 1 January 2000 as more recent studies include time-period where the prevalence of depression has increased dramatically. (3) they had follow up period <1 year; (4) major dietary patterns were examined without separate analysis of fruit and/or vegetables; (5) the studies were published in languages other than English; and if the populations included in the studies (6) had pre-existing conditions (i.e., any health problems that exist at an earlier time, including depression); (7) they had specific nutritional needs; and (8) they were unique populations which are less likely to be representative of the general population (e.g., monks).

2.3. Search Strategy

The systematic review focused on peer-reviewed cohort studies published from 1 January 2000 to 31 August 2020. Prespecified search terms and Medical Subject Headings (MeSH) terms were utilised to identify potentially relevant articles from six databases, namely Medline, EMBASE, PreMedline, and PsycINFO via Ovid, CINAHL via EBSCO, and Scopus. Two reviewers (PNAD and MJ) conducted a comprehensive search using the following keywords: (a) type of food ('fruit' OR 'vegetable' OR 'FV'), (b) 'consumption' OR 'intake', (c) mental disorders ('depression' OR 'depressive disorder' OR 'depressive symptoms'), (d) population ('young people' OR 'young adults' OR 'adults'), and (e) study design ('longitudinal stud*' or 'cohort stud*'). Full details of the search strategy can be found in Supplementary Table S2.

2.4. Study Selection

All studies identified were imported into EndNote X9 citation management software (Thomson Reuters, Toronto, Ontario, Canada). At the first stage studies were verified and screened based on title and abstract by two reviewers (PNAD and MJ). At the second stage, all potentially relevant studies were independently screened and scrutinised for eligibility by three reviewers (PNAD, MJ, and SM). Any discrepancies were resolved by discussion between researchers. Reference lists of eligible studies were manually searched to identify any additional studies. The procedure of identification and screening process for selection of cohort studies is presented in Figure 1.

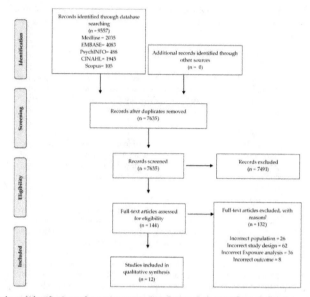

Figure 1. Flowchart of identification and screening process for selection of cohort studies exploring the association between fruit and vegetable intake and depressive symptoms in young people and adults aged 15–45 years.

2.5. Data Extraction

Data extraction was independently conducted by two reviewers (PNAD and MJ) and then validated by SM using a pre-determined data extraction table. Key study components were extracted including (1) characteristics of participants (age, gender, and country of origin), (2) study details (cohort assessed, number of participants, and follow up period), (3) outcome and exposure assessment methods (diet and depression), (4) main results (including β coefficients, OR, HR, 95% CI, and p values), and (5) confounding factors (including all models of adjustment).

2.6. Quality Assessment

Two researchers (PNAD and SM) independently appraised the study quality and risk of bias of each eligible studies using the Newcastle-Ottawa Scale (NOS) for cohort studies [49]. This framework used following criteria to categorise studies: Selection (scale from 0 to 4), comparability (scale from 0 to 2), and outcome (scale from 0 to 3). The overall score of each included study was used to categorise studies as: "very good" quality (8–9 NOS points), "good" quality (6–7 NOS points), "moderate" quality (4–5 NOS points), and "low" quality (0–3 NOS points) [50]. Differences in scores regarding the quality assessment were resolved by discussion and consensus between the two researchers.

3. Results

3.1. Search Results

A total of 9557 potentially relevant studies were identified using the search strategy on six electronic databases, (Medline = 2035, EMBASE = 4083, PsycINFO = 488, PreMedline = 901, CINAHL = 1945, and Scopus = 105) which was reduced to 7635 after removal of duplicates. After abstract and title screening in the first stage, 7491 studies were excluded leaving 144 full-text articles. Of the 144 studies that were screened in full-text publications for eligibility, 12 studies were deemed eligible and included in the qualitative synthesis [51–62]. No additional articles were retrieved from reference list searching. The flowchart in Figure 1 displays the process of selection. Those full-text studies which were deemed ineligible with reasons are reported in Supplementary Table S3.

3.2. Study Characteristics

Table 1 shows the study characteristics. Most of the included studies were conducted in European countries; three were based in the United Kingdom (UK) [53,55,60], one from France [57], one from Spain [62], and one from Sweden [54]. Three studies were conducted in the United States of America (USA) [56,59,61], and the remaining studies were each located in Japan [51], Canada [58], and Australia [52]. The earliest publication date was 2009 and the most recent 2020. Duration of the study follow-up period ranged from 2–14 years with the number of participants varying from 139 to over 45,000. The age ranges at baseline of some of the studies also included participants that were outside the 15–45 years age group, although they were recruited in this age range, as was the nature of the longitudinal cohort. One commentary study [52] was also included as an eligible study because it presented an extra evidence regarding depression and anxiety using the same cohort data from previous study conducted by the same authors [63]. In terms of analysis, one study analysed only vegetable intake [51], and one study exclusively analysed fruit intake [54], while the rest analysed both fruit and vegetable intake [52,53,55–62]. One study consisted of only female participants [59] while the rest comprised of individuals from both genders [51–58,60–62]. One study [60] reported raw data from only female participants as results in the male participants were not significant. This study also separated analysis into measurements taken at two different time points: 5-years and 10-years.

3.3. Dietary Measures

Semi-quantitative food frequency questionnaires were used to assess diet and fruit and vegetable intake in four studies [51,59,60,62], two studies used country specific food frequency questions, one from the National Cancer Institute [61] and the other from the USA Centres for Disease Control and Prevention [58]. Multiple 24-h recalls were used in another [57], a 4d diet diary in one study [55], and self-reported questionnaires in four studies [52–54,56]. When looking at the analysis of exposure, three analysed the impact fruits and vegetables had independently on depression [56,60,62], five combined fruits and vegetables in their analysis [52,55,57,58,61], one looked specifically at only flavonoid containing foods which included fruits and vegetables [59], and one study analysed both the impact of fruit and vegetable together and separately [53].

3.4. Depression Measures

Depression assessment methods varied between studies. The most commonly used screening instruments to measure depressive symptomatology were the General Health Questionnaire (GHQ-12) [51,53,54], and the Centre for Epidemiologic Studies Depression Scale (CESD), two studies used CESD-20 [57,60], and one used both CESD-20 and CESD-10 in different waves of the study [56]. Other instruments included Composite International Diagnostic Interview-Short Form (CIDI-SF) [58], and the Moods and Feelings Questionnaire (MFQ) [55]. One study used a Short Form (SF-12) Health Survey [61], and was included as it had some measures of depression and mental health. Two studies included questions about diagnosis of depression and/or use of antidepressant medication [52,62] and another used a combination of methods across different assessment time periods [59].

Table 1. Characteristics of included studies.

Reference/Country/Year	Participant Characteristics (Age Range, Mean Age at Baseline (SD), Gender)	Study Characteristics (Number of Participants, Follow-Up Period)	Cohort	Dietary Assessment Method (Recall Period)	Depression Assessment Method (Analysis Assessment)
Choda et al. [51] Japan, 2020	Age range at baseline: 35–69 y Age mean: Participants with a GHQ score ≥ 4 is 50.1 (9.1); Participants with a GHQ score < 4 is 52.9 (9.5) Gender (female): ~50%	4701 ~5 y (Daiko) ~6 y (Shizuoka)	The Japan Multi-Institutional Collaborative Cohort (J-MICC), the Daiko Study and the Shizuoka area	A validated short FFQ (46 food items) (over the past years)	The 12-item General Health Questionnaire (the GHQ-12) (psychological distress and social dysfunction factors)
Mujcic and Oswald [52] Australia, 2019	Age range: ≥15 y Age mean:-ᵃ Gender (female):-ᵃ	7108 2 y	The Household, Income, and Labour Dynamics in Australia (HILDA) Survey	Short questions on usual intake and frequency intake: "how many days in a usual week do you eat fruit?" and "how many days in a usual week do you eat vegetables?" "On a day when you eat fruit, how many serves of fruit do you usually eat?" and "On a day when you eat vegetables, how many serves of vegetables do you usually eat?" [63]	"Have you ever been told by a doctor or nurse that you have any of long-term health conditions listed below? Please only include those conditions that have lasted or are likely to last for six months or more: Depression/Anxiety"
Ocean et al. [53] UK, 2019	Age range at baseline: 15–104 y Age mean: 47.1 Gender (female):-ᵃ	Over 45,000 6 y	The UK Household Longitudinal Study (UKHLS)	Short questions on portion intake: "on a day when you eat fruit or vegetables, how many portions of fruit and vegetables in total do you usually eat?"	The 12-item General Health Questionnaire (the GHQ-12) (psychological distress and social dysfunction factors)
Winzer et al. [54] Sweden, 2018	Age range: 18–29 y Age mean:-ᵃ Gender (female): 61.8%	1704 ~12 y	The Stockholm Public Health Cohort (SPHC)	Short questions on frequency intake: How often do you eat Fruit and berries (an apple, an orange, a banana, a glass of juice, grapes, strawberries)?	The 12-item General Health Questionnaire (the GHQ-12) (psychological distress and social dysfunction factors)
Winpenny et al. [55] UK, 2018	Age range at baseline: 14 y Age mean: 14.5 (0.3) Gender (female): 60%	603 3 y	The ROOTS study	A 4d diet diary (two weekdays and two weekend days)	The Moods and Feelings Questionnaire (MFQ) (depressive symptoms)
Hoare et al. [56] USA, 2018	Age range at baseline: 12–18 y Age mean at baseline: 15.9 (1.7) Age mean at follow up: 28.9 (1.7) Gender (female):-ᵃ	3696 ~14 y	Add Health	Short questions on frequency intake: "How often did you eat fruit or drink fruit juice yesterday?" The same item with response options was asked for vegetable consumption (previous day)	The Centre for Epidemiologic Studies Depression Scale CES-D 20 (Wave 1) CES-D 10 (Wave 4) (depressive symptoms)

Table 1. Cont.

Reference/Country/Year	Participant Characteristics (Age Range, Mean Age at Baseline (SD), Gender)	Study Characteristics (Number of Participants, Follow-Up Period)	Cohort	Dietary Assessment Method (Recall Period)	Depression Assessment Method (Analysis Assessment)
Collin et al. [57] France, 2016	Age range: 35–60 y Age mean: 49.5 (6.2) Gender (female): 56.2%	3328 11 y *	Supplementation en Vitamines et Mineraux AntioXydants (SU.VI.MAX)	Multiple (3–6) 24-h recalls (Usual intake)	CES-D 20 (Chronic or recurrent depressive symptoms)
Kingsbury et al. [58] Canada, 2016	Age range: 18–104 y Age mean: 44.16 (18.41) Gender (female): 52.8%	8353 Continuous every 2 y (1994/1995–2010/2011)	Canadian Longitudinal Survey	Food frequency questions: From the fruit and vegetable module in the behavioural risk factor surveillance system of the USA Centres for Disease Control and prevention (Usual intake)	CIDI-SF (Major depression) K6 (Distress)
Chang et al. [59] USA, 2016	Age ** range: 36–55 y Age mean: ~46.3 (4.6) Gender (female): 100%	36,658 10 y	Nurses' Health Study II ** (NHSII)	Semi-quantitative FFQ (130 food items) (Previous years usual intake)	MHI-5 (1993, 1997) Antidepressant use (1997) Doctor diagnosis (2001) (Depression)
Akbaraly et al. [60] UK, 2013	Age range at baseline: 35–55 y Age at initial measurement for this analysis: 39–64 y Gender (female): 25.1%	4215 (5 y) 4053 (10 y)	Whitehall II study, UK civil servants	Semi-quantitative FFQ (127 food items) (Previous years usual intake)	CES-D 20 or/and use of antidepressant medication (Depressive symptoms)
Chai et al. [61] USA, 2010	Age range: ≥18 y Age mean: 55.3 (15.5) Gender (female): 74.1%	139 2 y	Multiethnic sample of adults living in Hawaii	Food Frequency questions: National Cancer Institute fruit and vegetable questionnaire. (Previous months intake)	SF-12 Health Survey (SF-12)
Sanchez-Villegas et al. [62] Spain, 2009	Age range at baseline: 18–104 y Age mean male: 42.7 (13.3) [64] Age mean female: 35.1 (10.7) [64] Gender (female): ~58.4%	10,094 4.4 y	The Seguimiento Universidad de Navarra' Study cohort, alumni of the University in Spain (SUN cohort)	Semi-quantitative FFQ (136 food items) (Usual intake)	Positive response to "Have you ever been diagnosed as having depression by a medical doctor" or/ and who reported the habitual use of antidepressant drugs. (Clinical depression)

Abbreviations: SD; standard deviation, y; years, UK; United Kingdom, FFQ; food frequency questionnaire, CES-D; Centre for Epidemiologic Studies Depression Scale, SU.VI.MAX; Supplementation en Vitamines et Mineraux AntioXydants, USA; United States of America, CIDI-SF; Composite International Diagnostic Interview-Short Form, K6; Kessler psychological Distress Scale, SUN; Seguimiento Universidad de Navarra/University, NHS; Nurses' Health Study, 4d; 4day, MHI-5; 5-item mental health index, and QOL; quality of life. * Follow up 1996–1997 to 2007–2009. ** Study included data from NHS as well however characteristics were described independently and thus those from the NHSII are only presented in this table. ^a This information was not provided in the publication.

3.5. Quality Assessment

The Newcastle-Ottawa Scale for cohort studies was used to assess the study quality. The detailed results of the quality assessment are seen in Supplementary Table S4, where the total score for the Newcastle-Ottawa Scale is given. One study was deemed as "very good" quality [58], the majority of studies (n = 9) categorised as "good" quality [51–56,59,60,62], and two studies were categorised as "moderate" quality [57,61]. Most of the studies failed to meet the requirements on ascertainment of exposure and assessment of outcome because written self-report was used to collect the exposure and outcome information, which was likely to introduce bias. Furthermore, the studies of moderate quality [57,61] only received one point each for selection and outcome criteria. No studies were excluded on the basis of their quality assessment.

3.6. Outcomes

A pooling of the results was not possible because the differences in the ways that analysis were conducted, and outcomes were reported and thus, results were tabulated and described qualitatively. Key results are presented in Table 2 and the summary of findings in Table 3.

3.6.1. Impact of Fruit and Vegetable Intake on Depressive Symptoms

Two good quality studies and one moderate quality study explored the impact of fruit and vegetable intake on depressive symptoms [54,56,59]. Two studies used the CES-D instrument [57,60], and one study used the MFQ to assess depressive symptoms [55]. At an individual study level, in the 5-year analysis of the Whitehall II cohort [60], a greater consumption of both vegetables and fruit decreased the odds of recurrent depressive symptoms in women while no significant results were seen in men. In the 10-year analysis an improvement or maintenance of vegetable intake was associated with reduced odds of recurrent depressive symptoms in women, while women whose consumption decreased over the same time frame had higher odds of recurrent depressive symptoms. Similarly, an increased fruit intake decreased the odds of depression development in the 10-year analysis, however, no significant association was observed when women maintained or decreased fruit intake. In contrast, Winpenny et al. [55] reported no prospective association between fruit and vegetable intake at age 14 years and depression symptomatology at age 17 years after adjusting for risk factors, such as depressive symptoms at baseline, socio-economic status, physical activity, and total energy intake. Similarly, the finding from the Supplementation en Vitamines et Mineraux Antioxydants (SU.VI.MAX) study [57] illustrated that adherence to the French nutrition guidelines resulted in a decrease in depressive symptom development due to an overall healthy diet. This was ascertained by comparing the guidelines score without inclusion of fruit and vegetables and the result was still protective.

Four studies investigated the impact of fruit and/or vegetable intake independently on more general measures of depressive symptoms including mental health measures [51,53,54,61]. Three good quality studies used the GHQ-12 [51,53,54] and one moderate study used the SF-12 Health Survey [61]. In the Japan Multi-Institutional Collaborative Cohort (J-MICC) study [51], an inverse association between vegetable intake and a GHQ score $\geq$ four was not significant after controlling for confounders. In contrast to that, the study from Sweden highlighted that daily consumption of fruit and berries was a substantial determinant to predict stability in mental health among the 18–29 age group [54]. Similar results were observed in a longitudinal UK study [53] which showed the importance of both frequency and quantity of intake of fruit and vegetables on good mental health. It was highlighted that daily consumption of fruit and/or vegetable (at least one portion) contributed to maintenance of good mental health. Moreover, frequent vegetable consumption had a more substantial effect on mental health than frequent consumption of fruit. One moderate quality study that assessed emotional and mental health found that fruit and vegetable consumption had no significant association with mental health, and the results indicated that increased physical activity had a positive association with better mental health, irrespective of fruit and vegetable consumption [61].

Table 2. Description of exposure, outcome and key results of studies.

Ref	Exposure	Outcome	Fruit and Vegetable	Key Results - Fruit	Key Results - Vegetable
[51]	Vegetable intake (frequency)	Mental Health (GHQ-12)	N/A	N/A	Model 2 p-trend = 0.291 Ref: Lowest quartile of exposure (Q1) OR: Q2 = 1.20 (0.95–1.50) OR: Q3 = 0.98 (0.77–1.25) OR: Q4 = 1.21 (0.95–1.55)
[52]	Fruit and vegetable (portions/day) Reverse causality Diagnosed with depression/anxiety	Depression/Anxiety (Doctor diagnosis) Fruit and vegetable	$\beta = -0.0041$ (−0.008, −0.001) $p = 0.017$ ** $\beta = -0.0718$ (−0.174, 0.031) $p = 0.170$	N/A N/A	N/A N/A
[53]	Fruit and vegetable (portions/day) Days each week eat fruit (frequency) Days each week eat vegetables (frequency)	Well-being (GHQ-12)	Specification (3) = 0.133 *** (0.0245)	Specification (4) Ref: Never 1–3 days = 0.259 *** (0.0896) 4–6 days = 0.423 *** (0.0989) Every day = 0.613 *** (0.0982)	Specification (4) Ref: Never 1–3 days = 0.518 *** (0.171) 4–6 days = 0.803 *** (0.175) Every day = 0.925 *** (0.177)
[54]	Consumption of fruit and berries (frequency)	Mental Health (GHQ-12)	N/A	N/A	p-trend = 0.071 Ref: Rare consumption of fruit and berries OR: Daily consumption = 1.39 (1.05–1.84) ** OR: Weekly consumption = 1.25 (0.94–1.67)
[55]	Fruit and vegetables (servings/day)	Depressive symptoms (MFQ)	Model 3: β = 0.14 (−0.15, 0.43) Model 3 (male): β = 0.06 (−0.32, 0.44) Model 3 (female): β = 0.21 (−0.22, 0.64)	N/A	N/A
[56]	Fruit consumption (quantity/day) Vegetable consumption (quantity/day)	Depression (CES-D 10 and CES-D 20)	N/A	Model 3 (pro) In males results Ref: No fruit consumption OR: Once = 0.72 (0.46, 1.11) OR: Twice + = 0.71 (0.47, 1.07) In females results Ref: No fruit consumption OR: Once = 0.92 (0.63, 1.33) OR: Twice + = 0.73 (0.62, 1.26)	Model 3 (pro) In males results Ref: No vegetable consumption OR: Once = 1.07 (0.72, 1.57) OR: Twice + = 1.02 (0.66, 1.56) In females results Ref: No vegetable consumption OR: Once = 0.74 (0.54, 1.02) OR: Twice + = 0.80 (0.57, 1.12)
[57]	PNNS-GS [a] without Fruits and vegetables	Depressive symptoms (CES-D 20)	Excluding fruits and vegetables OR: 0.84 (0.77, 0.91) *** $p = <0.0001$ When adjusted for fruit and vegetable intake the PNNS-GS score remained statistically significant	N/A	N/A
[58]	Fruit and vegetable intake (daily frequency) Fruit and vegetable intake (daily frequency)	Depression (CIDI-SF) Distress (K6)	Model 2 (dep): β = −0.03 (−0.05 to −0.01) Model 3 (dep): β = 0.001 (−0.03 to 0.04) Model 2 (dis): β = −0.03 (−0.05 to −0.01) Model 3 (dis): β = 0.02 (−0.01 to 0.04)	N/A	N/A

Table 2. Cont.

Ref	Exposure	Outcome	Key Results - Fruit and Vegetable	Key Results - Fruit	Key Results - Vegetable
[58]	Inverse association Depression Distress	Fruit and vegetable intake Fruit and vegetable intake	Model 2: β = −0.27 (−0.42 to −0.11) Model 3: β = −0.10 (−0.22 to 0.02) Model 2: β = −0.02 (−0.03 to −0.01) Model 3: β = 0.01 (−0.01 to 0.02)	N/A	N/A
[59]	Citrus fruit and juice combined (servings/day) Citrus fruit (servings/day) Onions (servings/day)	Depression (MHI−5, antidepressant use, doctor diagnosis)	N/A	Citrus fruit and juice combined $p = <0.0001$ *** Ref: Lowest quintile of exposure (Q1) HR: Q2 = 0.94 (0.85, 1.05) HR: Q3 = 0.89 (0.78, 1.02) HR: Q4 = 0.85 (0.75, 0.97) HR: Q5 = 0.82 (0.74, 0.91) Citrus fruit $p = 0.001$ *** Ref: Lowest quintile of exposure (Q1) HR: Q2 = 0.93 (0.88, 0.99) HR: Q3 = 0.91 (0.86, 0.96) HR: Q4 = 0.97 (0.83, 1.13) HR: Q5 = 0.87 (0.75, 1.01)	Onions $p = 0.25$ Ref: Lowest quintile of exposure (Q1) HR: Q2 = 1.00 (0.94, 1.06) HR: Q3 = 0.98 (0.92, 1.05) HR: Q4 = 0.96 (0.89, 1.02) HR: Q5 = 0.99 (0.89, 1.09)
[60]	5−year analysis (Phase 7) Vegetable intake (servings/day) Fruit intake (servings/day)	Depressive symptoms (CES−D 20 or/and use of antidepressant medication)	N/A	OR: −0.68 [b] (0.58, 0.97) (Model 3)	OR: −0.65 [b] (0.51, 0.88) (Model 3)
[60]	10−year analysis (Phase 9) Vegetable intake (servings/day) Fruit intake (servings/day)	Depressive symptoms (CES−D 20 or/and use of antidepressant medication)	N/A	Women's results Ref: Those who maintained low OR: Maintaining = −0.60 [b] (0.40, 1.01) OR: improving = −0.30 [b] (0.25, 0.60) Ref: Those who maintained high OR: Decreasing = −1.55 [b] (0.90, 3.01) (NS)	Women's results Ref: Those who maintained low OR: Maintaining = −0.50 [b] (0.30, 0.90) OR: Improving2 = −0.45 [b] (0.27, 0.91) Ref: Those who maintained high OR: Decreasing = −2.6 [b] (1.35, 5.35)
[61]	Fruit and vegetable intake (servings/day)	Quality of Life (SF−12)	MCS scores $p > 0.05$ at all-time points (T1−T7) Correlation co-efficient ranged from: −0.06 to 0.13	N/A	N/A
[62]	Fruits and nuts (grams/day) Vegetables (grams/day)	Depression (doctor diagnosis or antidepressant use)	N/A	p trend = 0.007 *** Ref: Lowest quintile of exposure (Q1) HR: Q2 = 0.69 (0.53−0.91) HR: Q3 = 0.67 (0.51−0.88) HR: Q4 = 0.69 (0.52−0.91) HR: Q5 = 0.61 (0.45−0.82) Merged Q3−Q5: 0.67 (0.54−0.84)	p trend = 0.81 Ref: Lowest quintile of exposure (Q1) HR: Q2 = 0.88 (0.67−1.17) HR: Q3 = 0.87 (0.66−1.16) HR: Q4 = 0.94 (0.71−1.25) HR: Q5 = 0.93 (0.69−1.24)

Abbreviations: N/A; not available, AHEI; Alternate healthy eating index, SD; standard deviation, OR; odds ratio, Ref; reference, NS; not significant, PNNS-GS; French Programme National Nutrition Sante´-Guidelines Score, Q; quartile/quintile, Dep; depression, Dis; distress, HR; hazard ratio, MDP; Mediterranean dietary pattern, Pro; prospective, MCS; Mental component summary score, CES-D; Centre for Epidemiologic Studies Depression Scale, GHQ; General Health Questionnaire, CIDI-SF; Composite International Diagnostic interview- Short form, K6; Kessler psychological Distress Scale, MHI-5; 5-item Mental health index, SF-12; The 12-item Short Form Survey, and MFQ; Mood and Feelings Questionnaire. ** $p < 0.05$. *** $p < 0.01$. [a] Refer to Appendix A. [b] Raw data not reported- only graphically represented estimate provided.

Table 3. Summary of the study findings accompanied by the quality assessment based on the total score for the Newcastle–Ottawa Scale.

Ref	Summary	Quality
[51]	Vegetable consumption was not associated with GHQ score before or after adjustment of confounders using prospective logistic regression. Adequate consumption of certain nutrients and foods may lead to better mental health in Japanese adults.	Good
[52]	Individuals who increased fruit and vegetable intake from 0 to 8 portions/day were on average 3.2% points less likely to experience depression or anxiety within the next 24 months. Fruit and vegetable consumption may help to protect against future risk of clinical depression and anxiety. There is no decisive evidence on whether the current rate of depression or anxiety predicts higher or lower fruit and vegetable consumption in the future.	Good
[53]	Mental well-being responds in a dose-response fashion to increases in both the quantity and the frequency of fruits and vegetables consumed. Increasing one's consumption of fruit and vegetables by one portion (on a day where at least one portion is consumed) leads to a 0.133-unit increase in mental well-being ($p < 0.01$). The more often fruit and vegetables are consumed in a week, the more likely individuals have a higher mental well-being.	Good
[54]	Consuming fruit and berries on a daily basis were considered as a determinant for stable mental health. Having healthy food intake, demonstrated by consuming fruit and berries, was one of six determinants to predict stability in mental health.	Good
[55]	Fruit and vegetable consumption at age 14 years were not significantly associated with depressive symptoms at age 17 years based on prospective logistic regression. Diet quality was not significantly associated with depressive symptoms.	Moderate
[56]	Fruit and vegetable consumption could be a protective factor against adult depression. Fruit consumption among males and vegetable consumption among females were prospectively associated with a reduced risk of adult depression in unadjusted models (Model 1). The association between vegetable consumption and reduced risk of adult depression among females remained significant after adjusted for adolescent depression, but not in fully adjusted model (Model 3).	Good
[57]	Higher adherence to the French nutritional guideline assessed by PNNS-GS [a] was associated with a lower likelihood of chronic or recurrent depressive symptoms. This association was not driven by any specific component of the PNNS-GS (including Fruit and vegetables) but was a result of an overall healthy diet.	Moderate
[58]	A greater fruit and vegetable consumption at the initial measurement was associated with a lower risk of depression at the next. This association was evident in Model 2 adjustments however disappeared once obesity was included in the adjustment (Model 3). Similarly, a greater fruit and vegetable consumption at the initial measurement was associated with lower distress scores at the next; however, disappeared once social support smoking and physical activity were added to the model (Model 3). Inverse association showed that depression and distress at initial measurements predicted lower consumption of fruits and vegetables at the next measurement. These associations were no longer evident once social support, smoking and physical activity were added to the model.	Very Good
[59]	Citrus intake (fruit and juice) ≥2 servings/d was associated with an 18% reduction in depression risk. [b] Independently both citrus fruit and juice showed significant associations to a reduction in depression. This was true for moderate to high intakes of citrus fruit but only high intakes of juice. Onion intake was not associated with depression risk. Diet higher in flavonoids results in a moderate reduction in risk of depression- especially in older women.	Good
[60]	High consumption of fruits and vegetables was associated with lower odds of recurrent depression. Improvement in fruit and vegetable score led to lower odds of subsequent depressive symptoms compared to those who maintained low scores. Decrease in AHEI [a] score led to higher odds of depression in vegetables but not fruit. Improvement in fruit and vegetable score led to lower odds of subsequent depressive symptoms compared to those who maintained low scores. Decrease in AHEI score led to higher odds of depression in vegetables but not fruit.	Good
[61]	There was no significant association between MCS score and daily fruit and vegetable consumption. Increasing weekly physical activity levels was significantly associated with increasing MCS at all time points. Physical activity predictive of positive mental health irrespective of other behaviours such as fruit and vegetable intake and TV/video watching	Moderate
[62]	Greater adherence to the Mediterranean dietary pattern [a] resulted in more than a 30% reduction in depression development. Compared to participants with the lowest consumption fruit and nut those with the highest intake had a 39% decreased risk of developing depression. There was no significant association between vegetable intake and depression. Compared to participants with lowest consumption of legumes those with highest intake had a 27% decreased risk of developing depression.	Good

Abbreviations: AHEI; Alternate healthy eating index, PNNS-GS; French Programme National Nutrition Santé 'Guidelines Score, MCS; Mental component summary score, GHQ; General Health Questionnaire. [a] Refer to Appendix A. [b] This trend was consistent for both NHS and NHSII cohort.

3.6.2. Impact of Fruit and Vegetable Intake on Depression

One very good quality study and four good quality studies examined the association between fruit and vegetable intake and depression, of which four studies measured the depression doctors diagnosis or medication use [52,58,59,62], and one study used the CES-D instrument [56]. Two good quality studies reported the protective effect of fruit intake against risk of developing depression [59,62]. Moreover, a significant protective effect was observed from greater intakes of legumes and "fruits and nuts" [62]. Citrus fruits and juices were also shown to reduce the odds of depression in women from the Nurses' Health Study [59]. However, a greater intake of vegetables had no significant effect on the development of depression in individuals in the Seguimiento Universidad de Navarra (SUN) study [62]. The very good quality study showed fruit and vegetable intake not to be associated with depression development or distress after adjusting for the key confounders [58]. Contrastingly, Mujcic and Oswald [52] found an inverse association between fruit and vegetable consumption and the probability of being diagnosed with depression/anxiety within the next 24 months. An interesting finding in the Add Health cohort [56] was that the association between fruit consumption during adolescence and reduced odds of depression in adulthood was not significant after adjustment for adolescent depression. Contrary to that, consuming vegetables once a day was significantly related to reduced odds of adult depression among females after adjustment for adolescent depression, but not at higher intakes (twice or more a day). However, this association was substantially attenuated after further controlling for relevant confounders.

4. Discussion

This systematic review aimed to evaluate the association between fruit and vegetable intake and depressive symptoms in young people and adults aged 15–45 years. We identified 12 cohort studies from seven countries. Among six cohort studies which analysed the impact of combined fruit and vegetable consumption [52,53,55,57,58,61], only two studies demonstrated an inverse association with depressive symptoms [52,53]. Varying results were observed when the effects of fruit and vegetables were analysed separately. Among the five good quality studies which showed an inverse association between fruit consumption and depression after adjusting for key confounders [53,54,59,60,62], two good quality studies showed that the association was observed in women [59,60]. Two good quality studies showed an association between vegetable consumption and lower risk of development depression [53,60]. Two good quality studies showed no association between vegetable consumption and depression [51,62]. One very good quality study and one good quality study, although initially showing a significant association in unadjusted models, showed no association between fruit and vegetable intake and depression after adjustment for confounders, such as obesity, physical activity, and BMI [56,58]. These results suggest that fruit and vegetable independently may lead to different effects on mental health. Two moderate quality studies showed no association between fruit and vegetable intake and depression symptoms [57,61]. Two good quality studies reported possible gender effects, because there were different impacts of fruit and vegetable consumption on depression between women and men [56,60]. Although we are unable to make definite assertions, the evidence seems to be building that a possible association exists, and this may have implications for addressing the burden of mental illness in young people and adults aged 15–45 years.

A common finding across the 12 studies was the low intake of fruit and vegetables generally, and the failure to meet recommended guidelines. According to the Understanding Society study [53], 87% of 15–29 year-olds and 80% of 30–41 year-olds consumed fewer than five portions a day in the UK. Despite the low rate of adherence to guidelines, the study found that even small increases in the consumption patterns of individuals may translate into substantive positive effects for the well-being [53]. Furthermore, the more often fruits and vegetables are eaten in a week, the better mental well-being is likely to be. The study by Winzer et al. [54] for example concluded that consuming fruit and berries on daily basis is a determinant of stability in mental health in the 18–29 age group. Another study also illustrated that vegetable consumption once a day among women was prospectively associated with a reduced risk of adult depression although the association diminished after further adjustment for key confounders [56]. These findings indicate that even one portion of fruit and vegetable daily is likely to reduce the risk of depression in adults. It is notable that the frequency with which fruit and vegetables are consumed is crucial. An additional finding was that depression did not predict lower consumption of fruits and vegetables longitudinally [52,58].

The most salient findings were that the independent effects of fruits and vegetables on depression and depressive symptoms differed when analysed separately. The inverse relationship was more likely to be observed between fruit intake and depressive symptoms than vegetable intake. Such disparities were also seen in a study conducted in Australian middle-aged women [65]. A higher intake of fruits was seen to be protective of depressive symptoms in both cross sectional and longitudinal analyses whereas vegetables were only protective using cross sectional analyses. Authors from this study suggested that the discrepancy between the two food groups could be a result of differing chemical composition, whereby fruits tended to contain higher levels of antioxidants and anti-inflammatory components such as carotenoids, flavonoids, and resveratrol. While this is a possibility, it may also be hypothesised that in these studies the vegetable intake is not consumed in quantities high enough to see protective effects, or that the types of vegetables consumed in larger amounts do not contain the corresponding nutrients suggested to be protective. Therefore, further studies are required to observe the independent effects of fruit and vegetables on depression and depressive symptoms.

Interestingly, in two good quality studies, there was evidence of differences in the association according to gender [56,60]. The results demonstrated that vegetable consumption among females is inversely associated with future depressive symptoms. The association was attenuated in a US study by further adjustment for potential confounders [56], while the other remained significant [60]. In terms of fruit consumption, no significant association was observed in both genders in the US study [56], whereas an inverse association was significantly observed in women only in the Whitehall II study from the UK [60]. A plausible explanation for the gender differences, may be explained by psychosocial factors. According to Emanuel et al. [66], a gender difference in fruit and vegetable intake may be attributable to attitudes and perceived behavioural control. Women reported more favourable attitudes and perceived behavioural control towards fruit and vegetable intake than men.

While all studies adjusted for most key potential confounders, it is difficult to say with certainty that all confounding factors were accounted for, due to the complex nature of both depression and diet. For instance, the studies that showed protective effects against depression did not adjust for BMI in their analysis [53,54,60]. BMI has been shown to have a non-linear association with depression, whereby those who are underweight or obese tend to have higher odds of depression compared to individuals that are normal weight or overweight [67,68]. Thus, failure to adjust for BMI, despite adjustment for central obesity, may have obscured the effects observed in the Canadian longitudinal study [58]. Additionally, none of the included studies adjusted for fish intake in their analysis. Greater intakes of fish and omega-3 fatty acids have been associated with lower odds of depression development and thus could be an important confounding factor [69–71]. Not adjusting for all confounders may mean that the associations observed are a result of an unmeasured variable and thus not a true reflection of the association between exposure and outcome. This influence was evident in two included studies [56,58] where consuming vegetable once a day were shown to be protective against depression development in women until adjustments of age, household income, ethnicity, physical activity, and body mass index were made [56], and fruits and vegetables were shown to be protective against depression development until additional adjustments of social support, obesity, and smoking were made in Canadian longitudinal study [58].

Different measurement tools in exposure and outcome may also contribute to the current conflicting results. This may have contributed to the variations in results seen. There were large variations in the methods used to assess intake of fruits and vegetables. For example, four studies used serving size [55,59–61], while three studies used frequency of consumption [53,54,58], and another used meeting the national guidelines [51]. A study by Offringa et al. [72] illustrated that the total fibre content of vegetables consumed by 100-kcal portions was significantly higher compared to the total fibre content of vegetables consumed per serving. Therefore, this difference may interfere with the impact of vegetable consumption on predictive depressive symptoms. The dynamic and varying nature of diet means that there may be unavoidable errors in dietary measurements. Therefore, it is important to determine the strengths and weaknesses of the assessment methods used within each study. Reporting bias may be present in all studies as food intake relies on the participants' recall ability and assumption that reported intake close to the true intake. Participants may be inclined to over emphasize their usual intake towards including healthier food choices as this appears more socially desirable [73]. Often, the use of a sensitivity analysis would tend to negate the effects of misreporting, however, none were conducted in any of the included studies. Validation of the dietary assessment method is therefore necessary to ensure the results are accurate. Despite the individual dietary assessment methods having their own limitations, most of the included studies used validated tools. Similarly, different instruments across the studies were used for defining depression, which not limited to clinical diagnosis or antidepressant use.

In spite of the use of validated instruments, such as the CES-D and GHQ-12, using different ways of scoring and cut-off points might affect the results [4]. According to Fried [74], lack of content overlap among common depression scales may pose a threat to the generalisability and replicability of depression research. The results of depressive symptoms assessed with the CES-D are less likely to generalise to other depression scales due to idiosyncratic items and lack of overlap [74]. Each depression scale was developed for different purposes, for instance, the CES-D was developed specially to screen for depression in a general population setting [75]. Similarly, the GHQ-12 was widely used in the general population and non-psychiatric settings, however in terms of screening, it is not limited to identify depression, but also common mental disorders [76]. Significant results were observed when the screening of depression was using both self-reported depression scale and clinical diagnostic (doctor diagnosis or antidepressant use) [52,59,60,62]. Possibly, the differences in content between self-reported depression scale and clinician assessment may lead to lower the agreement on diagnosis of depression, which affect the results [77–79]. Therefore, the utilization of clinician assessment and self-reported depression scale in future studies is recommended to achieve the most accurate prediction of depression.

Existing literature reviews conducted on the diet–depression relationship have shown varying results. While some have illustrated positive effects around healthy dietary patterns and decreased risk of depression [10,12,24], others have detected no association [41]. Furthermore, in line with the results obtained from this review, most existing work recommended the need for additional research in this area, especially studies with cohort designs [40,42,80]. To address one of the methodological limitations in previous systematic reviews, the eligible studies were only those studies conducted with a longitudinal cohort design, with the hope of obtaining a clearer sequential relationship and stronger causal inferences between fruit and vegetable consumption and depression symptoms. However, a concrete conclusion is unable to be drawn. The lengths of follow-up duration varied across the studies but overall, no difference effects were found. It is nevertheless noteworthy that the unadjusted potential confounders and different measurement tools probably have stronger effects on contradictory results.

There have been few randomised controlled trials (RCT) which have assessed the relationship between fruit and vegetable intake and depression. Although experimental evidence is the best study design to assess causal effects, most RCTs are very short term and are performed in populations with existing illness. For example, an intervention study to increase fruit and vegetable consumption in young adults with low fruit and vegetable consumption indicated that fruit and vegetable consumption improved several aspects of psychological well-being [16] but this was only carried out over 14 days. Two RCTs showed significant reductions in depressive symptoms in young adults with depression symptoms after a brief diet intervention [81,82]. However, the diet intervention was designed to comply with healthy diet recommendations, and fruit and vegetables were consumed along with other food groups. Additionally, the target populations were young adults with depression, which differed with the healthy population in our systematic review.

This study looks solely at the impact of fruits and vegetables because few systematic reviews [42] examined its impact on depression and most of them have examined the impact of dietary patterns on depression. We chose this option because findings will be able to be translated more readily into recommendations for whole foods. In addition, this review exclusively examined the association in young people and adults aged 15–45 years which is the age transition where most mental health issues arise.

Strengths and Limitations

The exclusive use of cohort studies poses both a limitation and strength to this review. The inclusion of only a single study design is a form of selection bias. However, by reviewing only cohort studies, the direction of causation is easier to infer as there is more likely to be a temporal association between exposure and outcome, provided subjects with the outcome at baseline are excluded from the analysis. Additional strengths of this review include the comprehensive nature of the search strategy, thorough quality analysis and the large sample sizes seen in 10 of the 12 studies may have led to a higher statistical power to ascertain an effect. Importantly, this systematic review provides results of the independent effects of fruit and vegetable separately enabling us to recognize any differential effects which adds to the research base on this topic. To our knowledge, this is the first systematic review of cohort studies to evaluate the association between fruit and vegetable intake and depressive symptoms in young people and adults aged 15–45.

The strict inclusion criteria for our systematic review resulted in only 12 studies being eligible for review and between studies, there were also considerable methodological differences which made direct comparisons challenging. Most of included studies used dietary recall to assess fruit and vegetable consumption. This methodology might be liable to recall bias although it has higher precision in assessing dietary intakes. In terms of exposure assessment, measurement of fruit and/or vegetable consumption varies from grams/day, to portions, serving sizes, quantity, and frequency. Different instruments were used across studies to assess depressive symptomatology, which not limited to clinical diagnosis or antidepressant use. Inconsistency in the outcome measures resulted in different definitions of depression or depressive symptomatology, which also might affect the results. Further, the validity of results may be limited because the age range in majority of studies were slightly extended outside of young people and adults aged 15–45 years. Other limitations include language bias, as studies published in languages other than English were excluded and publication bias may be present.

5. Conclusions

Despite a paucity of cohort studies, this study complements existing work evaluating the evidence on the impact of fruit and vegetable consumption on depression. Unique aspects of this systematic review include the exclusive use of cohort studies, specifically in young people and adults aged 15–45. Our findings highlight the potential importance of the association between fruit and vegetable consumption and depressive symptoms in young people and adults aged 15–45 years. There is inconclusive evidence on the effect fruits and vegetables have on reducing the odds of developing depression and depressive symptoms. More robust evidence is needed to address the specific aspects of diet that could prevent the development of depression. Thus, we recommend the diet–depression relationship be examined in well-designed prospective cohorts as well as randomised controlled trials. With the evidence building there is potential to inform public policy and add positive mental health outcomes to an already extensive list of reasons as to why people should prioritise a healthy diet.

Supplementary Materials: The following are available online at https://www.mdpi.com/1660-4601/18/2/780/s1, Table S1: Inclusion and exclusion criteria for study designs; Table S2: Full electronic search strategy applied for Medline, Embase, and PsycInfo; Table S3: Justification of exclusion at full text screening; Table S4: The Newcastle–Ottawa Scale results.

Author Contributions: S.M. and M.A.-F. conceptualised the study including the scope and preliminary search terms. P.N.A.D. and M.J. identified and screened potentially relevant studies. P.N.A.D., M.J., and S.M. screened and scrutinised full-text studies for eligibility. P.N.A.D. and M.J. undertook data extraction which was validated by S.M., P.N.A.D. and S.M. appraised the study quality and risk of bias. P.N.A.D. and M.J. wrote the paper, then S.M and M.A.-F. reviewed and edited the paper. All authors read and approved the final manuscript. All authors have read and agreed to the published version of the manuscript.

Funding: This research received no external funding.

Institutional Review Board Statement: Not applicable.

Informed Consent Statement: Not applicable.

Data Availability Statement: Data sharing not applicable.

Acknowledgments: Thank you to Jeremy Cullis for his assistance with the search strategy and assistance with databases throughout the screening process.

Conflicts of Interest: The authors declare no conflict of interest.

Appendix A

Diet Types Explained

Alternate healthy eating index (AHEI): Alternate healthy eating index comprises of summing 9 component scores (fruit, vegetable, ratio of white meat (seafood and poultry) and red meat, trans fat, ratio of PUFA to SFA, total fibre, nuts and soy, alcohol consumption and long-term multivitamin use) where by a higher score corresponds to a healthier diet [60].

PNNS-GS: Based on the Program National Nutrition Sante' the PNNS-GS contains 13 dietary components. 8 of the components referred to meeting the food serving recommendations, while four of the components are markers of limited consumption for recommendations without providing quantified frequency. The final components helps estimate adherence to physical activity recommendations on a daily basis [83].

Mediterranean diet pattern (MDP): consists of 9 components: high ration of MUFA to SFA, moderate alcohol intake, high intake of legumes, high intake of cereal, high intake of fruit and nuts, high intake of vegetables, low intake of meat and meat products, moderate intake of milk and dairy products and high intake of fish. The score was positive for intake above the median for 6 components (MUFA/SFA ratio, legumes, cereal, fruit and nuts, vegetables or fish), and intake below the median for 2 components (meat and dairy). For alcohol, points were given if intake was within a sex specific range [62].

References

1. World Health Organization. Depression and Other Common Mental Disorders: Global Health Estimates. Available online: http://apps.who.int/iris/bitstream/10665/254610/1/WHO-MSD-MER-2017.2-eng.pdf?ua=1 (accessed on 28 July 2020).
2. Ferrari, A.J.; Charlson, F.J.; Norman, R.E.; Patten, S.B.; Freedman, G.D.; Murray, C.J.; Vos, T.; Whiteford, H.A. Burden of Depressive Disorders by Country, Sex, Age, and Year: Findings from the Global Burden of Disease Study. *PLoS Med.* **2013**, *10*, e1001547. [CrossRef] [PubMed]
3. Liu, Q.; He, H.; Yang, J.; Feng, X.; Zhao, F.; Lyu, J. Changes in the global burden of depression from 1990 to 2017: Findings from the Global Burden of Disease study. *J. Psychiatr. Res.* **2020**, *126*, 134–140. [CrossRef] [PubMed]

4. Saghafian, F.; Malmir, H.; Saneei, P.; Milajerdi, A.; Larijani, B.; Esmaillzadeh, A. Fruit and vegetable consumption and risk of depression: Accumulative evidence from an updated systematic review and meta-analysis of epidemiological studies. *Br. J. Nutr.* **2018**, *119*, 1087–1101. [CrossRef]
5. Bilsen, J. Suicide and Youth: Risk Factors. *Front. Psychiatry* **2018**, *9*, 540. [CrossRef] [PubMed]
6. Viner, R.M.; Ross, D.; Hardy, R.; Kuh, D.; Power, C.; Johnson, A.; Wellings, K.; McCambridge, J.; Cole, T.J.; Kelly, Y.; et al. Life course epidemiology: Recognising the importance of adolescence. *J. Epidemiol. Community Health* **2015**, *69*, 719–720. [CrossRef]
7. Vos, T.; Lim, S.S.; Abbafati, C.; Abbas, K.M.; Abbasi, M.; Abbasifard, M.; Abbasi-Kangevari, M.; Abbastabar, H.; Abd-Allah, F.; Abdelalim, A.; et al. Global burden of 369 diseases and injuries in 204 countries and territories, 1990–2019: A systematic analysis for the Global Burden of Disease Study 2019. *Lancet* **2020**, *396*, 1204–1222. [CrossRef]
8. World Health Organizanization. Mental Health and Substance Use. Available online: https://www.who.int/teams/mental-health-and-substance-use/suicide-data (accessed on 2 January 2021).
9. Lopresti, A.L.; Hood, S.D.; Drummond, P.D. A review of lifestyle factors that contribute to important pathways associated with major depression: Diet, sleep and exercise. *J. Affect. Disord.* **2013**, *148*, 12–27. [CrossRef]
10. Lassale, C.; Batty, G.D.; Baghdadli, A.; Jacka, F.N.; Sánchez-Villegas, A.; Kivimäki, M.; Akbaraly, T.N. Healthy dietary indices and risk of depressive outcomes: A systematic review and meta-analysis of observational studies. *Mol. Psychiatry* **2019**, *24*, 965–986. [CrossRef]
11. Altun, A.; Brown, H.; Szoeke, C.; Goodwill, A.M. The Mediterranean dietary pattern and depression risk: A systematic review. *Neurol. Psychiatry Brain Res.* **2019**, *33*, 1–10. [CrossRef]
12. Lai, J.S.; Hiles, S.; Bisquera, A.; Hure, A.J.; McEvoy, M.; Attia, J. A systematic review and meta-analysis of dietary patterns and depression in community-dwelling adults. *Am. J. Clin. Nutr.* **2013**, *99*, 181–197. [CrossRef]
13. Tarelho, L.; Duarte, M.; Melim, J.; Batista, A.; Almeida, S. Dietary Pattern and Mental Health: Review of Literature. *Eur. Psychiatry* **2016**, *33*, S517. [CrossRef]
14. Mason-D'Croz, D.; Bogard, J.R.; Sulser, T.B.; Cenacchi, N.; Dunston, S.; Herrero, M.; Wiebe, K. Gaps between fruit and vegetable production, demand, and recommended consumption at global and national levels: An integrated modelling study. *Lancet Planet. Health* **2019**, *3*, e318–e329. [CrossRef]
15. Slavin, J.L.; Lloyd, B. Health Benefits of Fruits and Vegetables. *Adv. Nutr.* **2012**, *3*, 506–516. [CrossRef] [PubMed]
16. Conner, T.S.; Brookie, K.L.; Carr, A.C.; Mainvil, L.A.; Vissers, M.C.M. Let them eat fruit! The effect of fruit and vegetable consumption on psychological well-being in young adults: A randomized controlled trial. *PLoS ONE* **2017**, *12*, e0171206. [CrossRef]
17. Saghafian, F.; Malmir, H.; Saneei, P.; Keshteli, A.H.; Hosseinzadeh-Attar, M.J.; Afshar, H.; Siassi, F.; Esmaillzadeh, A.; Adibi, P. Consumption of fruit and vegetables in relation with psychological disorders in Iranian adults. *Eur. J. Nutr.* **2018**, *57*, 2295–2306. [CrossRef]
18. Ju, S.-Y.; Park, Y.-K. Low fruit and vegetable intake is associated with depression among Korean adults in data from the 2014 Korea National Health and Nutrition Examination Survey. *J. Health Popul. Nutr.* **2019**, *38*, 1–10. [CrossRef]
19. Peltzer, K.; Pengpid, S. Dietary consumption and happiness and depression among university students: A cross-national survey. *J. Psychol. Afr.* **2017**, *27*, 372–377. [CrossRef]
20. Wu, S.; Fisher-Hoch, S.P.; Reininger, B.M.; McCormick, J.B. Association between fruit and vegetable intake and symptoms of mental health conditions in Mexican Americans. *Health Psychol.* **2018**, *37*, 1059–1066. [CrossRef]
21. Bhattacharyya, M.; Marston, L.; Walters, K.; D'Costa, G.; King, M.; Nazareth, I. Psychological distress, gender and dietary factors in South Asians: A cross-sectional survey. *Public Health Nutr.* **2013**, *17*, 1538–1546. [CrossRef]
22. Kim, T.-H.; Choi, J.-Y.; Lee, H.-H.; Park, Y. Associations between Dietary Pattern and Depression in Korean Adolescent Girls. *J. Pediatr. Adolesc. Gynecol.* **2015**, *28*, 533–537. [CrossRef]
23. Angelino, D.; Godos, J.; Ghelfi, F.; Tieri, M.; Titta, L.; Lafranconi, A.; Marventano, S.; Alonzo, E.; Gambera, A.; Sciacca, S.; et al. Fruit and vegetable consumption and health outcomes: An umbrella review of observational studies. *Int. J. Food Sci. Nutr.* **2019**, *70*, 652–667. [CrossRef] [PubMed]
24. Głąbska, D.; Guzek, D.; Groele, B.; Gutkowska, K. Fruit and Vegetable Intake and Mental Health in Adults: A Systematic Review. *Nutrition* **2020**, *12*, 115. [CrossRef] [PubMed]
25. Goh, C.M.J.; Abdin, E.; Jeyagurunathan, A.; Shafie, S.; Sambasivam, R.; Zhang, Y.; Vaingankar, J.A.; Chong, S.A.; Subramaniam, M. Exploring Singapore's consumption of local fish, vegetables and fruits, meat and problematic alcohol use as risk factors of depression and subsyndromal depression in older adults. *BMC Geriatr.* **2019**, *19*, 1–9. [CrossRef] [PubMed]
26. Tsai, A.C.; Chang, T.-L.; Chi, S.-H. Frequent consumption of vegetables predicts lower risk of depression in older Taiwanese-results of a prospective population-based study. *Public Health Nutr.* **2011**, *15*, 1087–1092. [CrossRef] [PubMed]
27. Payne, M.E.; Steck, S.E.; George, R.R.; Steffens, D.C. Fruit, Vegetable, and Antioxidant Intakes Are Lower in Older Adults with Depression. *J. Acad. Nutr. Diet.* **2012**, *112*, 2022–2027. [CrossRef]
28. Głąbska, D.; Guzek, D.; Groele, B.; Gutkowska, K. Fruit and vegetables intake in adolescents and mental health: A systematic review. *Rocz. Państwowego Zakładu Hig.* **2020**, *71*, 15–25. [CrossRef]
29. Khalid, S.; Williams, C.M.; Reynolds, S. Is there an association between diet and depression in children and adolescents? A systematic review. *Br. J. Nutr.* **2016**, *116*, 2097–2108. [CrossRef]

30. McMartin, S.E.; Jacka, F.N.; Colman, I. The association between fruit and vegetable consumption and mental health disorders: Evidence from five waves of a national survey of Canadians. *Prev. Med.* **2013**, *56*, 225–230. [CrossRef]
31. Palta, P.; Samuel, L.J.; Miller, E.R., 3rd; Szanton, S.L. Depression and Oxidative Stress: Results from a meta-analysis of observational studies. *Psychosom. Med.* **2014**, *76*, 12–19. [CrossRef]
32. Maes, M.; De Vos, N.; Pioli, R.; Demedts, P.; Wauters, A.; Neels, H.; Christophe, A. Lower serum vitamin E concentrations in major depression–Another marker of lowered antioxidant defenses in that illness. *J. Affect. Disord.* **2000**, *58*, 241–246. [CrossRef]
33. Miller, A.L. The methylation, neurotransmitter, and antioxidant connections between folate and depression. *Altern. Med. Rev.* **2008**, *13*, 216–226. [PubMed]
34. Jiménez-Fernández, S.; Gurpegui, M.; Díaz-Atienza, F.; Pérez-Costillas, L.; Gerstenberg, M.; Correll, C.U. Oxidative Stress and Antioxidant Parameters in Patients with Major Depressive Disorder Compared to Healthy Controls before and after Antidepressant Treatment: Results from a Meta-Analysis. *J. Clin. Psychiatry* **2015**, *76*, 1658–1667. [CrossRef] [PubMed]
35. Nowak, G. Zinc, future mono/adjunctive therapy for depression: Mechanisms of antidepressant action. *Pharmacol. Rep.* **2015**, *67*, 659–662. [CrossRef]
36. Fava, M.; Borus, J.S.; Alpert, J.E.; Nierenberg, A.A.; Rosenbaum, J.F.; Bottiglieri, T. Folate, vitamin B_{12}, and homocysteine in major depressive disorder. *Am. J. Psychiatry* **1997**, *154*, 426–428. [CrossRef] [PubMed]
37. Ghadirian, A.M.; Ananth, J.; Engelsmann, F. Folic acid deficiency and depression. *J. Psychosom. Res.* **1980**, *21*, 926–929. [CrossRef]
38. Reynolds, E.H. Folic acid, ageing, depression, and dementia. *BMJ* **2002**, *324*, 1512–1515. [CrossRef]
39. Rooney, C.; McKinley, M.; Woodside, J. A systematic review of the potential role of fruit and vegetables in depression. *Proc. Nutr. Soc.* **2016**, *75*, E162. [CrossRef]
40. Rahe, C.; Unrath, M.; Berger, K. Dietary patterns and the risk of depression in adults: A systematic review of observational studies. *Eur. J. Nutr.* **2014**, *53*, 997–1013. [CrossRef]
41. Murakami, K.; Sasaki, S. Dietary intake and depressive symptoms: A systematic review of observational studies. *Mol. Nutr. Food Res.* **2009**, *54*, 471–488. [CrossRef]
42. Sanhueza, C.; Ryan, L.; Foxcroft, D. Diet and the risk of unipolar depression in adults: Systematic review of cohort studies. *J. Hum. Nutr. Diet.* **2012**, *26*, 56–70. [CrossRef]
43. Australian Bureau of Statistics. Mental Health. Available online: https://www.abs.gov.au/statistics/health/health-conditions-and-risks/mental-health/latest-release (accessed on 15 October 2020).
44. National Intitute of Mental Health. Major Depression. Available online: https://www.nimh.nih.gov/health/statistics/major-depression.shtml (accessed on 15 October 2020).
45. Frech, A. Healthy behavior trajectories between adolescence and young adulthood. *Adv. Life Course Res.* **2012**, *17*, 59–68. [CrossRef] [PubMed]
46. Collins, S.; Dash, S.; Allender, S.; Jacka, F.; Hoare, E. Diet and Mental Health During Emerging Adulthood: A Systematic Review. *Emerg. Adulthood.* **2020**, 1–15. [CrossRef]
47. Australian Bureau of Statistics. National Survey of Mental Health and Wellbeing: Summary of Results. Available online: https://www.abs.gov.au/statistics/health/mental-health/national-survey-mental-health-and-wellbeing-summary-results/latest-release#articles (accessed on 2 January 2020).
48. Liberati, A.; Altman, D.G.; Tetzlaff, J.; Murlow, C.; Gøtzsche, P.C.; Ioannidis, J.P.A.; Clarke, M.; Devereaux, P.J.; Kleijnen, J.; Moher, D. The PRISMA Statement for Reporting Systematic Reviews and Meta-Analyses of Studies That Evaluate Health Care Interventions: Explanation and Elaboration. *PLoS Med.* **2009**, *6*, e1000097. [CrossRef] [PubMed]
49. Wells, G.A.; Shea, B.; O'Connell, D.; Peterson, J.; Welch, V.; Losos, M.; Tugwell, P. The Newcastle-Ottawa Scale (NOS) for Assessing the Quality of Nonrandomised Studies in Meta-Analyses. Available online: http://www.ohri.ca/programs/clinical_epidemiology/oxford.asp (accessed on 20 September 2020).
50. Lo, C.K.-L.; Mertz, D.; Loeb, M. Newcastle-Ottawa Scale: Comparing reviewers' to authors' assessments. *BMC Med. Res. Methodol.* **2014**, *14*, 45. [CrossRef]
51. Choda, N.; Wakai, K.; Naito, M.; Imaeda, N.; Goto, C.; Maruyama, K.; Kadomatsu, Y.; Tsukamoto, M.; Sasakabe, T.; Kubo, Y.; et al. Associations between diet and mental health using the 12-item General Health Questionnaire: Cross-sectional and prospective analyses from the Japan Multi-Institutional Collaborative Cohort Study. *Nutr. J.* **2020**, *19*, 1–14. [CrossRef]
52. Mujcic, R.; Oswald, A.J. Does eating fruit and vegetables also reduce the longitudinal risk of depression and anxiety? A commentary on 'Lettuce be happy'. *Soc. Sci. Med.* **2019**, *222*, 346–348. [CrossRef]
53. Ocean, N.; Howley, P.; Ensor, J. Lettuce be happy: A longitudinal UK study on the relationship between fruit and vegetable consumption and well-being. *Soc. Sci. Med.* **2019**, *222*, 335–345. [CrossRef]
54. Winzer, R.; Sorjonen, K.; Lindberg, L. What Predicts Stable Mental Health in the 18–29 Age Group Compared to Older Age Groups? Results from the Stockholm Public Health Cohort 2002–2014. *Int. J. Environ. Res. Public Health* **2018**, *15*, 2859. [CrossRef]
55. Winpenny, E.M.; Van Harmelen, A.-L.; White, M.; Van Sluijs, E.M.; Goodyer, I.M. Diet quality and depressive symptoms in adolescence: No cross-sectional or prospective associations following adjustment for covariates. *Public Health Nutr.* **2018**, *21*, 2376–2384. [CrossRef]
56. Hoare, E.; Hockey, M.; Ruusunen, A.; Jacka, F.N. Does Fruit and Vegetable Consumption During Adolescence Predict Adult Depression? A Longitudinal Study of US Adolescents. *Front. Psychiatry* **2018**, *9*, 581. [CrossRef]

57. Collin, C.; Assmann, K.E.; Andreeva, V.A.; Lemogne, C.; Hercberg, S.; Galan, P.; Kesse-Guyot, E. Adherence to dietary guidelines as a protective factor against chronic or recurrent depressive symptoms in the French SU.VI.MAX cohort. *Prev. Med.* **2016**, *91*, 335–343. [CrossRef] [PubMed]
58. Kingsbury, M.; Dupuis, G.; Jacka, F.; Roy-Gagnon, M.-H.; McMartin, S.E.; Colman, I. Associations between fruit and vegetable consumption and depressive symptoms: Evidence from a national Canadian longitudinal survey. *J. Epidemiol. Community Health* **2015**, *70*, 155–161. [CrossRef] [PubMed]
59. Chang, S.-C.; Cassidy, A.; Willett, W.C.; Rimm, E.B.; O'Reilly, E.J.; Okereke, O.I. Dietary flavonoid intake and risk of incident depression in midlife and older women. *Am. J. Clin. Nutr.* **2016**, *104*, 704–714. [CrossRef] [PubMed]
60. Akbaraly, T.N.; Sabia, S.; Shipley, M.J.; Batty, G.D.; Kivimäki, M. Adherence to healthy dietary guidelines and future depressive symptoms: Evidence for sex differentials in the Whitehall II study. *Am. J. Clin. Nutr.* **2013**, *97*, 419–427. [CrossRef] [PubMed]
61. Chai, W.; Nigg, C.R.; Pagano, I.; Motl, R.W.; Horwath, C.C.; Dishman, R.K. Associations of quality of life with physical activity, fruit and vegetable consumption, and physical inactivity in a free living, multiethnic population in Hawaii: A longitudinal study. *Int. J. Behav. Nutr. Phys. Act.* **2010**, *7*, 83. [CrossRef]
62. Sánchez-Villegas, A.; Delgado-Rodríguez, M.; Alonso, A.; Schlatter, J.; Lahortiga, F.; Majem, L.S.; Martínez-González, M.A. Association of the Mediterranean Dietary Pattern With the Incidence of Depression: The Seguimiento Universidad de Navarra/University of Navarra follow-up (SUN) cohort. *Arch. Gen. Psychiatry* **2009**, *66*, 1090–1098. [CrossRef]
63. Mujcic, R.; Oswald, A.J. Evolution of Well-Being and Happiness After Increases in Consumption of Fruit and Vegetables. *Am. J. Public Health* **2016**, *106*, 1504–1510. [CrossRef]
64. Seguí-Gómez, M.; De La Fuente, C.; Vázquez, Z.; De Irala, J.; A Martínez-González, M. Cohort profile: The 'Seguimiento Universidad de Navarra' (SUN) study. *Int. J. Epidemiol.* **2006**, *35*, 1417–1422. [CrossRef]
65. Mihrshahi, S.; Dobson, A.J.; Mishra, G.D. Fruit and vegetable consumption and prevalence and incidence of depressive symptoms in mid-age women: Results from the Australian longitudinal study on women's health. *Eur. J. Clin. Nutr.* **2015**, *69*, 585–591. [CrossRef]
66. Emanuel, A.S.; McCully, S.N.; Gallagher, K.M.; Updegraff, J.A. Theory of Planned Behavior explains gender difference in fruit and vegetable consumption. *Appetite* **2012**, *59*, 693–697. [CrossRef]
67. De Wit, L.; Van Straten, A.; Van Herten, M.; Penninx, B.; Cuijpers, P. Depression and body mass index, a u-shaped association. *BMC Public Health* **2009**, *9*, 14. [CrossRef] [PubMed]
68. Révah-Levy, A.; Speranza, M.; Barry, C.; Hassler, C.; Gasquet, I.; Moro, M.-R.; Falissard, B. Association between Body Mass Index and depression: The "fat and jolly" hypothesis for adolescents girls. *BMC Public Health* **2011**, *11*, 649. [CrossRef] [PubMed]
69. Bountziouka, V.; Polychronopoulos, E.; Zeimbekis, A.; Papavenetiou, E.; Ladoukaki, E.; Papairakleous, N.; Gotsis, E.; Metal-linos, G.; Lionis, C.; Panagiotakos, D. Long-term fish intake is associated with less severe depressive symptoms among elderly men and women: The MEDIS (MEDiterranean ISlands Elderly) epidemiological study. *J. Aging Health* **2009**, *21*, 864–880. [CrossRef] [PubMed]
70. Timonen, M.; Horrobin, D.; Jokelainen, J.; Laitinen, J.; Herva, A.; Räsänen, P. Fish consumption and depression: The Northern Finland 1966 birth cohort study. *J. Affect. Disord.* **2004**, *82*, 447–452. [CrossRef] [PubMed]
71. Li, F.; Liu, X.; Zhang, D. Fish consumption and risk of depression: A meta-analysis. *J. Epidemiol. Community Health* **2015**, *70*, 299–304. [CrossRef]
72. Offringa, L.C.; Stanton, M.V.; Hauser, M.E.; Gardner, C.D. Fruits and Vegetables Versus Vegetables and Fruits: Rhyme and Reason for Word Order in Health Messages. *Am. J. Lifestyle Med.* **2018**, *13*, 224–234. [CrossRef]
73. Hebert, J.R.; Clemow, L.; Pbert, L.; Ockene, I.S.; Ockene, J.K. Social Desirability Bias in Dietary Self-Report May Compromise the Validity of Dietary Intake Measures. *Int. J. Epidemiol.* **1995**, *24*, 389–398. [CrossRef]
74. Fried, E.I. The 52 symptoms of major depression: Lack of content overlap among seven common depression scales. *J. Affect. Disord.* **2017**, *208*, 191–197. [CrossRef]
75. Radloff, L.S. The CES-D Scale. A self-report depression scale for research in the general population. *Appl. Psychol. Meas.* **1977**, *1*, 385–401. [CrossRef]
76. Goldberg, D.P.; Blackwell, B. Psychiatric Illness in General Practice: A Detailed Study Using a New Method of Case Identification. *BMJ* **1970**, *2*, 439–443. [CrossRef]
77. Eaton, W.W.; Neufeld, K.; Chen, L.-S.; Cai, G. A Comparison of Self-report and Clinical Diagnostic Interviews for Depression: Diagnostic interview schedule and schedules for clinical assessment in neuropsychiatry in the Baltimore epidemiologic catchment area follow-up. *Arch. Gen. Psychiatry* **2000**, *57*, 217–222. [CrossRef] [PubMed]
78. Polaino, A.; Senra, C. Measurement of depression: Comparison between self-reports and clinical assessments of depressed outpatients. *J. Psychopathol. Behav. Assess.* **1991**, *13*, 313–324. [CrossRef]
79. Uher, R.; Perlis, R.H.; Placentino, A.; Dernovšek, M.Z.; Henigsberg, N.; Mors, O.; Maier, W.; McGuffin, P.; Farmer, A. Self-Report And Clinician-Rated Measures Of Depression Severity: Can One Replace The Other? *Depress. Anxiety* **2012**, *29*, 1043–1049. [CrossRef] [PubMed]
80. Quirk, S.E.; Williams, L.J.; O'Neil, A.; Pasco, J.A.; Jacka, F.N.; Housden, S.; Berk, M.; Brennan, S.L. The association between diet quality, dietary patterns and depression in adults: A systematic review. *BMC Psychiatry* **2013**, *13*, 175. [CrossRef] [PubMed]
81. Francis, H.; Stevenson, R.J.; Chambers, J.R.; Gupta, D.; Newey, B.; Lim, C.K. A brief diet intervention can reduce symptoms of depression in young adults—A randomised controlled trial. *PLoS ONE* **2019**, *14*, e0222768. [CrossRef]

82. Jacka, F.N.; O'Neil, A.; Opie, R.; Itsiopoulos, C.; Cotton, S.; Mohebbi, M.; Castle, D.; Dash, S.; Mihalopoulos, C.; Chatterton, M.L.; et al. A randomised controlled trial of dietary improvement for adults with major depression (the 'SMILES' trial). *BMC Med.* **2017**, *15*, 1–13. [CrossRef]
83. Estaquio, C.; Kesse-Guyot, E.; Deschamps, V.; Bertrais, S.; Dauchet, L.; Galan, P.; Hercberg, S.; Castetbon, K. Adherence to the French Programme National Nutrition Santé Guideline Score Is Associated with Better Nutrient Intake and Nutritional Status. *J. Am. Diet. Assoc.* **2009**, *109*, 1031–1041. [CrossRef]

Implications for the future research

The findings from the current systematic review have added to the literature on the diet-depression relationship. Although most included studies have overall good quality, well-designed prospective cohort studies are required to provide more robust results. For instance, relying on self-reported scales of depression symptoms will inevitably introduce some measurement errors due to biased responses. Therefore, the use of data linkage or datasets with doctor-diagnosed depression records is encouraged to assess depression symptoms along with self-reported scales. Furthermore, doctor diagnosis and self-reported scales have complementary roles in the assessment phase.

Similarly, different measurements of exposure led to inconsistency and may introduce bias. Fruit and vegetables are commonly reported based on portions or servings in daily intake, which may differ between countries. Using grams (g) for analytical purposes should be considered to standardise the measurement.

The current systematic review only included healthy populations, and the findings may not be directly generalisable to other populations, such as people with certain risk factors. Although potential confounders have been adjusted, only two studies (23, 24) have conducted a gender-stratified analysis on the association between fruit and vegetable consumption and depression symptoms. The findings suggest potential gender differences in this association. Therefore, effect modification may also explain the contradictory results in the current systematic review. Assessing effect modification in future studies may provide further insight into the diet-depression relationship, particularly other health behaviours (e.g. physical activity, drinking habit, and smoking).

References

1. Fleisher WP, Katz LY. Early onset major depressive disorder. Paediatr Child Health. 2001;6(7):444-8.
2. Klein DN, Glenn CR, Kosty DB, Seeley JR, Rohde P, Lewinsohn PM. Predictors of first lifetime onset of major depressive disorder in young adulthood. J Abnorm Psychol. 2013;122(1):1-6.
3. Copeland W, Shanahan L, Costello EJ, Angold A. Cumulative prevalence of psychiatric disorders by young adulthood: a prospective cohort analysis from the Great Smoky Mountains Study. Journal of the American Academy of Child and Adolescent Psychiatry. 2011;50(3):252-61.
4. Gustavson K, Knudsen AK, Nesvåg R, Knudsen GP, Vollset SE, Reichborn-Kjennerud T. Prevalence and stability of mental disorders among young adults: findings from a longitudinal study. BMC Psychiatry. 2018;18(1):65.
5. Sarris J, Thomson R, Hargraves F, Eaton M, de Manincor M, Veronese N, et al. Multiple lifestyle factors and depressed mood: a cross-sectional and longitudinal analysis of the UK Biobank (N = 84,860). BMC Med. 2020;18(1):354.
6. Furihata R, Konno C, Suzuki M, Takahashi S, Kaneita Y, Ohida T, et al. Unhealthy lifestyle factors and depressive symptoms: a Japanese general adult population survey. J Affect Disord. 2018;234:156-61.
7. Cabello M, Miret M, Caballero FF, Chatterji S, Naidoo N, Kowal P, et al. The role of unhealthy lifestyles in the incidence and persistence of depression: a longitudinal general population study in four emerging countries. Global Health. 2017;13(1):18-.
8. Bélair M-A, Kohen DE, Kingsbury M, Colman I. Relationship between leisure time physical activity, sedentary behaviour and symptoms of depression and anxiety: evidence from a population-based sample of Canadian adolescents. BMJ Open. 2018;8(10):e021119.
9. Levola J, Pitkanen T, Kampman O, Aalto M. The association of alcohol use and quality of life in depressed and non-depressed individuals: a cross-sectional general population study. Qual Life Res. 2018;27(5):1217-26.
10. Boden JM, Fergusson DM. Alcohol and depression. Addiction. 2011;106(5):906-14.
11. Sánchez-Villegas A, Toledo E, de Irala J, Ruiz-Canela M, Pla-Vidal J, Martínez-González MA. Fast-food and commercial baked goods consumption and the risk of depression. Public Health Nutr. 2012;15(3):424-32.
12. Saghafian F, Malmir H, Saneei P, Keshteli AH, Hosseinzadeh-Attar MJ, Afshar H, et al. Consumption of fruit and vegetables in relation with psychological disorders in Iranian adults. Eur J Nutr. 2018;57(6):2295-306.
13. Ju SY, Park YK. Low fruit and vegetable intake is associated with depression among Korean adults in data from the 2014 Korea National Health and Nutrition Examination Survey. J Health Popul Nutr. 2019;38(1):39.
14. Pengpid S, Peltzer K. Association between fruit/vegetable consumption and mental-health-related quality of life, major depression, and generalised anxiety disorder: A longitudinal study in Thailand. Iran J Psychiatr Behav Sci. 2019;13(2).
15. Slavin JL, Lloyd B. Health benefits of fruits and vegetables. Advances in nutrition. 2012;3(4):506-16.
16. Conner TS, Brookie KL, Carr AC, Mainvil LA, Vissers MCM. Let them eat fruit! The effect of fruit and vegetable consumption on psychological well-being in young adults: A randomised controlled trial. PLoS ONE. 2017;12(2):e0171206-e.
17. Saghafian F, Malmir H, Saneei P, Milajerdi A, Larijani B, Esmaillzadeh A. Fruit and vegetable consumption and risk of depression: accumulative evidence from an updated systematic review and meta-analysis of epidemiological studies. Br J Nutr. 2018;119(10):1087-101.

18. Liu X, Yan Y, Li F, Zhang D. Fruit and vegetable consumption and the risk of depression: A meta-analysis. Nutrition. 2016;32(3):296-302.
19. Rooney C, McKinley MC, Woodside JV. The potential role of fruit and vegetables in aspects of psychological well-being: a review of the literature and future directions. Proc Nutr Soc. 2013;72(4):420-32.
20. Głąbska D, Guzek D, Groele B, Gutkowska K. Fruit and vegetable intake and mental health in adults: A systematic review. Nutrients. 2020;12(1):115.
21. Khalid S, Williams CM, Reynolds SA. Is there an association between diet and depression in children and adolescents? A systematic review. Br J Nutr. 2016;116(12):2097-108.
22. Australian Institute of Health and Welfare. Burden of disease [Internet]. Canberra: Australian Institute of Health and Welfare; 2020 [updated 2021 February 18, cited 2021 March 3]. Available from: https://www.aihw.gov.au/reports/australias-health/burden-of-disease.
23. Akbaraly TN, Sabia S, Shipley MJ, Batty GD, Kivimaki M. Adherence to healthy dietary guidelines and future depressive symptoms: evidence for sex differentials in the Whitehall II study. Am J Clin Nutr. 2013;97(2):419-27.
24. Hoare E, Hockey M, Ruusunen A, Jacka FN. Does fruit and vegetable consumption during adolescence predict adult depression? A longitudinal study of US adolescents. Front Psychiatry. 2018;9:581.

Chapter 3:

Study 2: Fruit and vegetable consumption and depression symptoms in young women: results from 1973-78 cohort of the Australian Longitudinal Study on Women's Health

Rationale for the secondary analysis

The latest report from the Lancet Global Burden of Disease showed that depressive disorder is one of the leading causes of DALYs in young people aged 25-49 years (1). A number of epidemiological studies suggest that depression is more prevalent in women than in men (2-5). Therefore, several longitudinal studies investigated the association between diet and depression by conducting analyses separately in women and men (6, 7). The findings from the systematic review (Chapter 2) also observed the potential gender differences in the association between fruit and vegetable consumption and depression symptoms, with an inverse association that is more likely to be observed in women.

However, there have been relatively few studies examining the association between fruit and vegetable consumption and depression symptoms in women using a population-based cohort study (8, 9). This study will help fill the gap in the research pertaining to the effects of fruit and vegetable consumption in relation to depression symptoms among women generally, and young women in particular, using an Australian population-based cohort study.

The following manuscript describes the results of the differential effects of fruit and vegetable consumption in relation to depression symptom in young women from the 1973-78 cohort of the ALSWH. It has been written according to the European Journal of Nutrition's guidelines.

Article content

The article content was submitted at the European Journal of Nutrition. The appendices presented in this article can be found in Appendix 2 of the book.

Author contributions: GDM and SM designed the present study and framed the research question. PNAD conducted the statistical analysis, provided interpretation of results, and drafted the manuscript. SM provided suggestions and revised the manuscript. GDM guided the statistical analysis and provided critical input on the draft manuscript. All the authors approved the final version of the manuscript.

Fruit and vegetable consumption and depression symptoms in young women: results from 1973–78 cohort of the Australian Longitudinal Study on Women's Health

Putu Novi Arfirsta Dharmayani[1], Gita D. Mishra[2], Seema Mihrshahi[1]

[1] Department of Health Systems and Populations, Faculty of Medicine, Health and Human Sciences, Macquarie University, Sydney, NSW 2109, Australia;

[2] School of Public Health, University of Queensland, Brisbane, QLD 4006, Australia

Corresponding author:

Seema Mihrshahi

Department of Health Systems and Populations, Faculty of Medicine, Health and Human Sciences, Macquarie University, Sydney, NSW 2109, Australia

Email: seema.mihrshahi@mq.edu.au

Short title: Fruit and vegetable consumption and depression symptoms

This is the submitted version of the article: Dharmayani, P.N.A., Mishra, G.D. & Mihrshahi, S. Fruit and vegetable consumption and depression symptoms in young women: results from 1973 to 1978 cohort of the Australian Longitudinal Study on Women's Health. *European Journal of Nutrition* (2022). https://doi.org/10.1007/s00394-022-02926-8

Abstract

Purpose Growing evidence suggests that specific food groups may play an important role in improving mental health. However, very few studies explored the association between individual dietary factors and depression symptoms by following a large cohort of individuals over a long period. We examined the differential effects of fruit and vegetables in relation to depression symptoms over a 15-year follow up period in the 1973–78 cohort of the Australian Longitudinal Study on Women's Health.

Methods Fruit and vegetable consumption was assessed using short questions. The Center for Epidemiologic Studies Depression-10 scale with a cut off ≥ 10 indicated depressive symptoms. Multiple imputations with generalised estimating equations models were performed to estimate odds ratio of depression symptoms according to fruit and vegetable consumption.

Results A total of 4241 participants with a mean age of 27.6 (SD 1.45) years at baseline were followed up at five surveys (2003–2018). Fruit and vegetable intake (≥ 2 servings) was cross-sectionally associated with lower odds of depressive symptoms. In longitudinal analysis, higher intake of fruit (≥ 4 servings) and vegetable (≥ 5 servings) was consistently associated with lower odds of depressive symptoms, with a 25% lower odds (OR 0.75; 95% CI 0.57, 0.97; $p = 0.031$) and a 19% lower odds (OR 0.81; 95% CI 0.70, 0.94; $p = 0.007$) than consuming one serve or less fruit and vegetable respectively.

Conclusion These results suggest that a higher intake of fruit and vegetables was associated with a lower risk of depression symptoms over 15 years from a population-based prospective study of Australian women.

Keywords: fruit; vegetables; depression symptoms; young women; nutrition; diet

Introduction

Depression is a highly recurrent, debilitating, and prevalent mental disorder in the general population that can significantly hamper adaptive functioning [1]. With the number of individuals with depressive disorder steadily rising in most countries, it is predicted that major depressive disorder (MDD) will be the leading cause of disability and disease burden worldwide by 2030 [2,3]. According to recent findings from the Global Burden of Disease study, depression was the top-ranked cause of disability-adjusted life-years (DALYs) in the younger population [4]. A study by Rohde et al. [5] showed that emerging adulthood has the highest prevalence of MDD compared to other age groups.

A number of epidemiological studies concluded that the lifetime prevalence of depression in women is two-fold more prevalent than in men [6-8]. A meta-analysis representing data from 90 different nations showed a medium effect size of the gender difference in depressive symptoms and women having higher odds of depression symptoms compared with men [9]. There is a substantial economic burden related to health system spending for common mental disorders in several developed countries [10-12]. A recent systematic review and meta-analysis found considerably higher excess depression costs for total direct and indirect costs, notably in young people [13]. Thus, population-based prevention strategies are highly needed to reduce the incidence of depression and its economic burden.

A growing body of research suggests the potential influence of dietary patterns on common mental disorders. The role of diet in relation to health-related quality of life has been extensively investigated, with more positive associations observed with adherence to healthy dietary patterns and the Mediterranean diet [14,15]. Evidence from at least three systematic reviews found that both dietary patterns have also been associated with a greater reduce the risk of developing depression [16-18]. A common characteristic of both dietary patterns is higher intakes of fruit and vegetables. A meta-analysis of randomised controlled trials suggests greater benefits from dietary interventions by adhering to high-fibre and nutrient-dense alternatives, such as vegetables, to reduce depression symptoms among women samples [19]. Thus, the relationship between fruit and vegetable consumption and depression symptoms is an emerging area of research.

However, several systematic reviews found conflicting findings across age groups from observational evidence [20-24]. A differential effect of fruit and vegetables was reported in studies that examined the effects of fruit and vegetables separately on depression symptoms [25-27]. Our previous results from the Australian Longitudinal Study on Women's Health (ALSWH) study, for example, showed that greater consumption of fruit was associated with a reduced prevalence and incidence of depressive symptoms in mid-age women, whereas the effects of vegetables remained unclear [28].

Despite accumulating evidence, the associations of fruit and vegetable and depression symptoms remain relatively underexplored in young adults. Early adulthood is a period associated with low diet quality, and young adults are likely to be more susceptible to common mental disorders due to life transitions[24]. Evidence from longitudinal studies on fruit and vegetable consumption for preventing depression symptoms among young women is scarce. To address this gap, we investigate the association between fruit and vegetable consumption and depression symptoms in young women. Our study aims to examine the differential effects of fruit and vegetables in relation to depression symptoms over a 15-year follow-up in young women from the 1973–78 cohort of the ALSWH.

Methodology

Study sample and participants

The ALSWH is an ongoing prospective cohort study that aims to examine the associations between biological, psychological, social, and lifestyle factors and women's physical health and emotional well-being [29]. This study has collected health data from over 40,000 Australian women from three age cohorts, born in 1921–26, 1946–1951, and 1973–78 since 1996 [30]. Women were randomly recruited from the Medicare database in 1996, which covers all Australian citizens and permanent residents. In 2012–2013, the fourth cohort born in 1989–95 was included in the study. At baseline, participants have been shown to be broadly representative of Australian women in the same age group. Further information on the ALSWH is available on the official website (https://www.alswh.org.au/).

The sample for investigating the association between fruit and vegetable consumption and depression symptoms is drawn from the 1973–78 cohort. At the initial survey, a total of 14,247 women aged 18–23 completed the survey via mail. Self-administered questionnaires were sent to participants at approximately 3-year intervals until 2018 (survey 8). Details of study design, cohort and recruitment procedures have been described elsewhere [29]. This secondary analysis focuses on dietary data collected in the five survey waves from survey 3 in 2003 (age 25–30) until survey 8 in 2018 (age 40–45), where dietary intake short questions were administered in the questionnaires starting in 2003. Survey 3 was used as the baseline for the current study, and its response rate was 66.3% (n = 9,081). Survey 6 was excluded from analysis because dietary data was not collected.

Assessment of dietary intake

The daily intake of fruit and vegetable was assessed using the short questionnaires (Supplementary Table 1). Most short questions were asked the participants to report their daily intakes in serving size. A serve of fruit was equivalent to one medium piece or two small pieces of fruit, or a half cup of diced fruit, berries, or grapes, whereas a serve of vegetables was equivalent to half a cup (75 g) of cooked green or orange vegetables, or cooked dried or canned legumes, or sweet corn, or one cup of green leafy or raw salad vegetables [31]. Participants marked one only answer for each question according to their usual eating habits over the past 12 months.

Dietary intake data was collected using a food frequency questionnaire in Survey 3 and Survey 5, based on the validated Dietary Questionnaire for Epidemiological Studies Version 2 developed by the Cancer Council Victoria. Total energy and nutrient intakes were computed using Australian nutrient composition data from the NUTTAB 1995 [32]. The current study used the latest dietary intake data at survey 5 to calculate total energy intakes and fish consumption. Due to a skewed distribution, women were categorised into three groups based on their total fish consumption, namely never consuming fish, <30 g/day, and ≥30 g/day, for analysis.

Assessment of depression symptoms

The 10-item Center for Epidemiologic Studies Depression (CESD-10) scale was used to assess the presence of symptoms associated with depression over the previous week. This instrument is a shortened version of the CESD-20 scale, which was constructed and designed to measure depressive symptoms in the general adult population aged 18 or older [33]. Validation of CESD-10 against the CESD-20 using a cut-off of 10 or more has been demonstrated to minimise false-positive results with slight loss of sensitivity [34]. The CESD-10 contains a 10-item Likert scale questionnaire, and items are rated on a four-point Likert scale ranging from 0 ('rarely or none of the time') to 3 ('most or all of the time'). Scores range from 0 to 30, with higher scores indicating greater severity of depression symptoms. A cut-off ≥ 10 was used to indicate women having depression symptoms. Depression symptoms were treated as a binary (dichotomous) outcome variable in the analyses.

Assessment of covariates

A range of potential confounding variables was considered, and information on these was obtained at each survey. In addition, a number of sociodemographic, health behaviours, chronic diseases, and history of depression symptoms were included in the modelling of the association between fruit and vegetable consumption and depression symptoms.

Sociodemographic variables

Sociodemographic variables included area of residence (major cities; inner regional; outer regional/remote/very remote), ability to manage on available income (no difficulty/not too bad; difficult sometimes; very difficult/impossible), the highest level of education (high school or less; trade/college; university), marital status (married/*de facto*; single; separated/divorced/widowed), and having a child (no; yes). These variables were reported at each survey.

Health behaviours

Smoking status

Smoking status was categorised based on the Australian Institute of Health and Welfare [35] as a non-smoker, ex-smoker, irregular smoker, weekly smoker, and daily smoker. Alcohol consumption was classified according to National Health and Medical Research Council [36] criteria (non-drinker, low-risk drinker, rarely drinks, risky drinker, and high-risk drinker). As very few women were classified as 'high-risk drinkers', they were combined with the 'risky drinker' category.

Physical activity

Physical activity was self-reported at each survey. Participants reported on the frequency and duration of physical activities, such as walking briskly, moderate leisure activity, vigorous leisure activity, and vigorous household or garden chores, in the last week. Based on self-reported information, the amount of each activity was calculated using minutes of metabolic equivalents of task (MET-min) per week and physical activity was then categorised as 'nil/sedentary' (< 40 MET-min/week), 'low' ($40 \leq$ MET < 600 min/week), 'moderate' ($600 \leq$ MET $< 1,200$ min/week), and 'high' ($\geq 1,200$ MET-min/week) [37,38].

Body Mass Index

Body Mass Index (BMI) was calculated as self-reported weight (kg) divided by the square of self-reported height (m) and categorised as 'acceptable weight' ($18.5 \leq$ BMI < 25), 'underweight' (BMI < 18.5), 'overweight' ($25 \leq$ BMI < 30), and 'obese' (BMI ≥ 30).

History of chronic disease

Participants self-reported a range of medical conditions at each survey. In the current study, individuals who provided a positive response on short questions "in the last 3 years, have you been diagnosed or treated for: ..." with any of the following conditions were considered to have a chronic disease: heart disease, hypertension, and diabetes.

History of depression

Depression symptoms were self-reported and participants were determined to have a history of depression if they met any of the following criteria: (a) provided a positive response on the following question at survey 2 "Have you ever been told by a doctor that you have depression in the last 4 years?" or (b) reported having the CESD-10 scores which equal to 10 or more at survey 2 or 3.

Statistical analysis

The present analysis included participants who had complete data on fruit and vegetable consumption and the CESD-10 score across the surveys (n = 4,241). Baseline characteristics were described by calculating their frequencies as percentages for binary and categorical variables, and means with standard deviation (SD) for continuous variables. Characteristics of participants at baseline were compared using the Chi-square test for binary and categorical covariates, and *t-test* for normally distributed continuous covariates.

The primary analysis used multiple imputations in conjunction with generalised estimating equations (GEE) models to examine the associations between fruit and vegetable consumption and depression symptoms. Multivariate imputation by chained equations (MICE) was performed to handle missing data in confounders [39,40]. Sampling variability from the imputation process can be reduced by increasing the number of imputed datasets (at least 20) [41]. Therefore, MICE was used to impute missing data on covariates with m=20 chains run for 20 iterations, with a logistic regression model for a binary variable, an ordered logistic regression for ordinal variables, and multinominal logistic regression for a nominal variable. The GEE regression models estimate the average effects over 15 years, accounting for within-participants correlation at all five surveys.

The total of the CESD-10 scores was dichotomised using the cut-off $\geq$ 10 to determine whether depression symptoms were present or not (0 = no depression symptoms, 1 = depression symptoms were present). In order to measure the daily servings, fruits were measured categorically, with three categories: $\leq$ 1 serve/day; 2-3 serves/day; $\geq$ 4 serves/day. Similarly, vegetables were classified into three categories: ≤ 1 serve/day; 2-4 serves/day; ≥ 5 serves/day. Models were adjusted for time-dependent variables reported at each survey, including area, ability to manage available income, marital status, having a child, smoking status, alcohol consumption, physical activity, BMI, and history of chronic diseases. Total energy intake and fish consumption were measured using the food frequency questionnaire data from survey 5, and the highest level of education at survey 8 was also added in the models. Further adjustment for the history of depression (survey 1–3) was also included in models to examine the longitudinal association. Age and gender were not included in the models because all participants were women aged 25–30 at the current study baseline. The final analyses included 21,205 observations for a total of 4,241 participants.

To test the robustness of our findings, a complete case analysis (listwise deletion) with the GEE model was performed, which omitted participants who had missing data on any of the variables used in the analysis. In addition, characteristics were compared with participants included in the analysis and excluded due to missing data on confounders. This analysis included 12,650 observations for a total of 2,531 participants who have completed data in the five survey waves. All analyses were conducted with STATA software version 16 (IBM Corp, Armonk, New York, USA) using a two-sided 5% level of significance.

Results

Descriptive characteristics

The analysis included a total of 4,241 participants representing 46.7% (4,241/9,081) of the total participants at baseline (Supplementary Fig. S1). These participants had complete data for daily intake of fruit and vegetable and the CESD-10 scores. Most of the characteristics of these participants differed from participants who were excluded in the analysis due to missing data on exposure and outcome of interest, except for age and history of chronic diseases (Table 1). Participants who were excluded in the analysis because of missing dietary information and the CESD-10 were more likely to have higher score in the CESD-10, be separated/divorced/widowed, have lower educational attainment, have difficulty in managing on income, have a child, be a daily smoker, less likely to physically active, be a drinker, and be obese.

A total of 1,281 participants reported having depression symptoms at least once across the surveys. Of these participants, 141 participants (3.3% of total) consistently showed symptoms of depression in the five survey waves (survey 3–8). A total of 2,136 (50.4%) participants showed no depression symptoms in any surveys. The prevalence of depressive symptoms in the sample over time was moderately stable, ranging from 19.6% to 23.2%. There were 769 (18.1% of total) new cases of depression symptoms during the 15-year follow-up period from survey 3 (2003) to survey 8 (2018) after excluding the 1,607 who had a history of depression from survey 1 to survey 3.

Table 2 describes the proportions of fruit and vegetable consumption by women from each survey. The prevalence of women consuming the recommended daily intakes of fruit and vegetables fluctuated across surveys. In terms of fruit consumption, approximately 40% of women consumed at least two servings daily. The prevalence of women consuming the recommended servings of vegetables considerably low throughout the surveys. Overall, few women ate the recommended daily intake of fruit and vegetables, ranging from 3.4% to 11.6% across surveys.

Cross-sectional analysis of fruit and vegetable consumption and depression symptoms

Table 3 presents the GEE analysis of cross-sectional associations between fruit and vegetable consumption and depression symptoms at each survey. Consuming fruit and vegetables were associated with lower odds of depressive symptoms after adjustment for energy intake, total fish consumption, and sociodemographic variables (Model 2). These associations remained strong even after health behaviours, BMI, and history of chronic diseases were included in the analysis (Model 3). The lowest odds in depression symptoms was observed among participants who consumed at least four servings of fruit each day with a 24% lower odds (OR 0.76; 95% CI 0.60, 0.96, p = 0.024) than participants who consumed one serve or less fruit. There was also a 21% lower odds among participants who consumed five or more servings of vegetables per day (OR

0.79; 95% CI 0.69, 0.91, p = 0.001) than participants who consumed one serve or less vegetable. Covariates associated with decreased odds of depression symptoms were having a child, low-risk drinking, and engaging with at least a low level of physical activity.

Longitudinal analysis of fruit and vegetable consumption and depression symptoms

Similar results were observed in longitudinal analysis with GEE models (Table 4). Higher fruit consumption (≥ 4 servings) was consistently associated with lower odds of depression symptoms among women who consumed at least four servings of fruit (OR 0.75; 95% CI 0.57, 0.97; $p = 0.031$) than those consuming one serve or less of fruit in the fully adjusted model (Model 4). Also, significant associations were observed in vegetable consumption and lower odds of depression symptoms among women who consumed 2-4 servings of vegetables (OR 0.85; 95% CI 0.76, 0.95; $p = 0.003$) and five servings or more vegetables (OR 0.81; 95% CI 0.70, 0.94; $p = 0.007$) than those consuming one serve or less of vegetable. The longitudinal association between consuming 2-3 servings of fruit and lower odds of depression symptoms was consistent after controlling for sociodemographic variables (Model 3). However, the association was attenuated after health behaviours, BMI, and history of chronic disease were introduced in the analysis (Model 4). Several covariates (difficulty in managing on income, being single, separated/divorced/widowed, a daily smoker, a risky/high-risk drinker, overweight, or obese) were significantly associated with increased odds of depression symptoms. On the other hand, having a child and engaging with at least a low level of physical activity were associated with decreased odds of depression symptoms.

Complete case analysis

Complete case analysis included 2,531 women in the analysis, excluding 1,710 women because of missing confounders (Supplementary Table 2). Most missing data was due to BMI (8.8%) at the baseline, history of chronic diseases (6.8%) in survey 5, and physical activity status (6.5%) in survey 8. Women included in the complete case analysis were more likely to live in major cities, have higher educational attainment, be less likely to have a child, and consume lower fish intake at the baseline. However, the mean of the CESD-10 scores did not differ between these groups.

The complete case analysis of higher consumption of fruit (≥ 4 servings) and vegetables (≥ 5 servings) did not alter the primary results in both cross-sectional and longitudinal after adjusting for covariates. Although consuming 2-3 servings of fruits lower odds of depression symptoms in the cross-sectional and longitudinal analyses, the associations were weak. Similarly, the association between consuming 2-4 servings of vegetables and depression symptoms was attenuated in longitudinal analysis (Supplementary Table 3).

Discussion

The present study provided evidence that higher intakes of fruit and vegetables (≥ 4 serving and ≥ 5 servings, respectively) were consistently associated with lower odds of depression symptoms over 15 years in Australian women in multiple imputation analysis and complete-case analysis. To our knowledge, this is the first study to provide evidence of the association between fruit and vegetable consumption and depression symptoms among young women over a 15-year follow-up.

We confirmed that a very low proportion of the sample population adheres to the recommended daily servings of fruit and vegetables, ranging from 3.4% to 11.6% across the surveys. This finding is common in population-based studies. For example, according to the Understanding Society study in the UK [42], only 13% of adults aged 15-29 and 20% of those aged 30-41 consumed the recommended daily intakes of fruit and vegetables. Furthermore, the rate of adherence to recommended amounts of vegetables was low among adults in three south Asian countries, with the highest rate was approximately 14% in Bangladesh, 7% in India, and 3% in Nepal based on data extracted from the World Health Survey [25].

Our cross-sectional findings are consistent with existing literature [43-46], which shows fruit and vegetable consumption (≥ 2 servings) was cross-sectionally associated with a lower risk of depression symptoms in young women. In alignment with our longitudinal findings, the evidence for sex differentials in the Whitehall II study showed that fruit and vegetables were independently associated with decreased odds of recurrent depression symptoms in women over 5 years [47]. Therefore, the authors suggested a long-term beneficial effect of adherence to the Alternative Healthy Eating Index (AHEI) to prevent depression symptoms due to specific nutrients provided by fruit and vegetables, such as high folate levels antioxidants. Similarly, a study conducted by Ocean et al. [42] found a dose-response effect between fruit and vegetable consumption and subjective well-being and highlighted the importance of increasing the quantity and frequency of fruit and vegetables consumed to increase mental well-being.

The findings of this study are generally in agreement with a recent systematic review and meta-analysis that found consumption of fruit and vegetable separately was associated with a lower risk of depression in adults based on the pooled relative risks in cross-sectional and cohort studies [48]. Likewise, a recent multi-national study concluded that inadequate fruit and vegetable consumption was associated with an increased likelihood of depression symptoms among adolescents in 25 low- and middle-income countries [49].

Our findings are somewhat different from the previous findings from the 1946–51 cohort of the ALSWH that found a reduction in the prevalence and incidence of depression symptoms with at least two servings of fruit, whereas the effects of vegetables were unclear [28]. We found a weak association between depression symptoms and women who consumed 2-3 servings of fruits (OR 0.94; 95% CI 0.87, 1.02; $p = 0.152$) than women consuming one serve or less fruit. Conversely, we found vegetable consumption at least two servings daily was significantly associated with lower odds of depression symptoms than participants consuming one serve or less vegetable in longitudinal analysis in the 1973–78 cohort of the ALSWH. Similar to our study, there was no observed association with fish consumption [28].

Several observational studies have shown mixed results on associations between fruit and vegetable consumption and depression symptoms. Reasons for this discrepancy may have been because of the effects of factors, such as smoking, physical activity, alcohol, and BMI [16,43,50,51]. For instance, a longitudinal study of US adolescents [43] showed a promising association between fruit consumption and depression with minimal adjustment for some covariates, but the association was attenuated after adjusting for BMI. Similarly, Winpenny et al. [50] reported that the association between fruit and vegetable consumption and depression was subsequently attenuated after controlling for behavioural covariates such as physical activity, smoking level, and alcohol consumption.

Further complicating matters, the associations between diet and depression symptoms are complex and plausibly bidirectional [51,52]. A longitudinal community survey in Australia found evidence of reverse causality between dietary patterns and depression [53]. Likewise, findings from the Invecchiare in Chianti Study found depression symptoms were associated with 3-year decreases in vegetable consumption but not in fruit consumption [54]. The underlying mechanisms of reverse causality are not clear, but it has been suggested that emotional eating is one factor accounting for the relationship between depression symptoms and unhealthy food choices, including lower intake of fruit and vegetables [55]. Emotional eating is considered as a coping strategy in response to negative emotions, such as depression and anxiety, in which may lead to changes in eating behaviour [55,56].

Plausible mechanisms

There are a number of concepts have been proposed to explain the mechanisms of action linking fruit and vegetable consumption with depression symptoms. The majority of findings are centred on the specific nutrients within fruit and vegetables, which influence psychological well-being [57]. Payne et al. [58] suggested that naturally occurring folate in foods, such as fruit and vegetables, may be more beneficial for preventing depression than dietary supplements and food fortification. The mechanisms proposed for their association have been linked to B vitamins because of their effects on single-carbon metabolism and their role in the synthesis of neurotransmitters, including serotonin, other monoamine neurotransmitters, and catecholamines [59,60]. Furthermore, the critical role of B vitamins in brain function is demonstrated by a number of neuropsychiatric symptoms commonly associated with deficiencies in any of the B vitamins, including folate and vitamin B_{12} [60,61]. A recent study found that the relationship between dietary patterns and depression mediated by serum levels of folate and vitamin B_{12} [62].

High concentrations of antioxidants in fruits and vegetables also present a promising link to psychological well-being. Depleted non-enzymatic antioxidants are considered to be the causative factors for oxidative stress, which may exhibit the development of major depressive disorder in the long term [63]. A recent study compiled a list of fresh fruits and vegetables which have the potential to prevent chronic human diseases [64]. Among fruits, berries have high antioxidants and phytochemicals such as flavonoids, tannins, and lignans [64]. In alignment with this finding, two cross-sectional studies found that berries have been inversely associated with depressive symptoms [65,66]. With regard to vegetables, broccoli, carrot, tomato, pea, and sweet pepper are vegetables with rich sources of phytochemical α-carotene and antioxidant β-carotene [64].

Strengths and Limitations

The strengths of our study include the use of data from a large population-based prospective cohort with repeated measurements of fruit and vegetable consumption, depression symptoms, and other health-related behaviours over 15 years. In addition, the assessment of depression symptoms utilised a validated and tested CESD-10 scale. We also adjusted for key confounders such as sociodemographic, lifestyle factors, body mass index, history of chronic disease, and other aspects of diet (total energy intake and fish consumption), which may reduce unmeasured residual confounding. Multiple imputation by chained equations was performed to improve the statistical power by imputing missing values, which is common in large datasets. Additionally, a complete case analysis was also presented to compare the results.

Our findings should also be interpreted in light of several limitations. First, almost half of the women had missing data in fruit and vegetable consumption and the CESD-10, which may introduce selection bias. In addition, we omitted the outcome variable from the imputation procedure. Some criticisms of the usage of MICE are that it does not have the same theoretical justification as other imputation approaches, and the imputation process unacceptably slow when the dataset contains many variables (e.g. several nominal categorical variables imputed by multinominal logistic regression) [67]. Furthermore, due to the exclusion of Survey 6 from the analysis, the direction of the odds of depression symptoms may bias the results towards the null.

The assessment method using self-report of both dietary intake and depression symptoms may be subject to reporting bias. In addition, inconsistency on short questions and answer choices used to measure the daily serving of fruit and vegetables over time may be prone to measurement error and confounding.

Although the history of depression prior to and at the baseline was adjusted for in the longitudinal analysis, the possibility of reverse causation may exist due to its observational nature. Finally, unmeasured residual confoundings (e.g., psychosocial factors) that are associated with depression symptoms may have introduced bias. Depression symptom in the current study is not reflective of clinical depression.

Conclusion

Our findings demonstrate that higher consumption of fruit and vegetables was associated with a lower risk of depression symptoms over a 15-year in young women from a population-based prospective study in Australia. Our results also support the evidence that fruit and vegetable consumption could be an important predictor of depression symptoms. To increase confidence in study findings, replication of the results in other populations is necessary. Improving dietary patterns to include more fruit and vegetables may be an essential component of strategies to prevent depression.

Supplementary material

For supplementary material/s referred to in this article, please visit XXXXX

Declarations

Acknowledgements

The research on which this paper is based was conducted as part of the Australian Longitudinal Study on Women's Health by the University of Newcastle and the University of Queensland. We are grateful to the Australian Government Department of Health for funding, to the study team and to all participants for their valuable contribution to this project. We are also grateful to Professor Janaki Amin and Associate Professor Peter Petocz for constructive and expert feedback on the statistical analysis.

The ALSWH is funded by the Australian Government Department of Health. P.N.A.D. was supported by the International Macquarie University Research Excellence Scholarship (iMQRES) from Macquarie University. G.D.M is supported by NHMRC principal fellowship (APP1121844). The funder had no role in the design, analysis or writing of this article.

Conflict of interest

The authors declare no conflict of interest.

Availability of data and material

Data are available from the Research Centre for Gender, Health, and Ageing (RCGHA) at the University of Newcastle and School of Public Health at the University of Queensland on request.

Author's contributions

G.D.M. and S.M. designed the present study and framed the research question. P.N.A.D. conducted the statistical analysis, provided interpretation of results, and drafted the manuscript. S.M. provided suggestions and revised the manuscript. G.D.M. guided the statistical analysis and provided critical input on the draft manuscript. All the authors approved the final version of the manuscript.

Ethical approval

The ALSWH has obtained ethics approval from the University and the University of Queensland, and the written informed consent is obtained for every survey. The use of the ALSWH data has been approved by the publications, analyses, and sub-studies committee of the ALSWH (EoI#A397) by the Research Centre for Gender, Health, and Ageing (RCGHA) at the University of Newcastle and School of Public Health at the University of Queensland.

References

1. Park EH, Jung MH (2019) The impact of major depressive disorder on adaptive function: A retrospective observational study. Medicine 98 (52):e18515. doi:10.1097/MD.0000000000018515
2. Yang L, Zhao Y, Wang Y, Liu L, Zhang X, Li B, Cui R (2015) The effects of psychological stress on depression. Curr Neuropharmacol 13 (4):494-504. doi:10.2174/1570159x1304150831150507
3. World Health Assembly (2012) Global burden of mental disorders and the need for a comprehensive, coordinated response from health and social sectors at the country level: report by the Secretariat. World Health Organization, Geneva
4. Vos T, Lim SS, Abbafati C et al. (2020) Global burden of 369 diseases and injuries in 204 countries and territories, 1990–2019: a systematic analysis for the Global Burden of Disease Study 2019. The Lancet 396 (10258):1204-1222. doi:10.1016/s0140-6736(20)30925-9
5. Rohde P, Lewinsohn PM, Klein DN, Seeley JR, Gau JM (2013) Key characteristics of major depressive disorder occurring in childhood, adolescence, emerging adulthood, adulthood. Clin Psychol Sci 1 (1):10.1177/2167702612457599. doi:10.1177/2167702612457599
6. Kuehner C (2017) Why is depression more common among women than among men? The Lancet Psychiatry 4 (2):146-158. doi:10.1016/S2215-0366(16)30263-2
7. de Graaf R, ten Have M, van Gool C, van Dorsselaer S (2012) Prevalence of mental disorders and trends from 1996 to 2009. Results from the Netherlands Mental Health Survey and Incidence Study-2. Soc Psychiatry Psychiatr Epidemiol 47 (2):203-213. doi:10.1007/s00127-010-0334-8
8. Picco L, Subramaniam M, Abdin E, Vaingankar JA, Chong SA (2017) Gender differences in major depressive disorder: findings from the Singapore Mental Health Study. Singapore Med J 58 (11):649-655. doi:10.11622/smedj.2016144
9. Salk RH, Hyde JS, Abramson LY (2017) Gender differences in depression in representative national samples: meta-analyses of diagnoses and symptoms. Psychol Bull 143 (8):783-822. doi:10.1037/bul0000102
10. Australian Institute of Health and Welfare (2021) Mental health services in Australia. AIHW. https://www.aihw.gov.au/reports/mental-health-services/mental-health-services-in-australia/report-contents/expenditure-on-mental-health-related-services. Accessed 25 February 2021
11. Jesulola E, Micalos P, Baguley IJ (2018) Understanding the pathophysiology of depression: From monoamines to the neurogenesis hypothesis model - are we there yet? Behavioural Brain Research 341:79-90. doi:https://doi.org/10.1016/j.bbr.2017.12.025
12. Roehrig C (2016) Mental disorders top the list of the most costly conditions in the united states: $201 billion. Health Affair 35 (6):1130-1135. doi:10.1377/hlthaff.2015.1659

13. König H, König HH, Konnopka A (2020) The excess costs of depression: a systematic review and meta-analysis. Epidemiology and Psychiatric Sciences 29:e30. doi:10.1017/S2045796019000180
14. Milte CM, Thorpe MG, Crawford D, Ball K, McNaughton SA (2015) Associations of diet quality with health-related quality of life in older Australian men and women. Exp Gerontol 64:8-16. doi:https://doi.org/10.1016/j.exger.2015.01.047
15. Vajdi M, Farhangi MA (2020) A systematic review of the association between dietary patterns and health-related quality of life. Health and Quality of Life Outcomes 18 (1):337. doi:10.1186/s12955-020-01581-z
16. Lai JS, Hiles S, Bisquera A, Hure AJ, McEvoy M, Attia J (2014) A systematic review and meta-analysis of dietary patterns and depression in community-dwelling adults. Am J Clin Nutr 99 (1):181-197. doi:10.3945/ajcn.113.069880
17. Lassale C, Batty GD, Baghdadli A, Jacka F, Sanchez-Villegas A, Kivimaki M, Akbaraly T (2019) Healthy dietary indices and risk of depressive outcomes: a systematic review and meta-analysis of observational studies. Mol Psychiatry 24 (7):965-986. doi:https://dx.doi.org/10.1038/s41380-018-0237-8
18. Altun A, Brown H, Szoeke C, Goodwill AM (2019) The Mediterranean dietary pattern and depression risk: a systematic review. Neurology, Psychiatry and Brain Research 33:1-10. doi:https://doi.org/10.1016/j.npbr.2019.05.007
19. Firth J, Marx W, Dash S, Carney R, Teasdale SB, Solmi M, Stubbs B, Schuch FB, Carvalho AF, Jacka F, Sarris J (2019) The effects of dietary improvement on symptoms of depression and anxiety: a meta-analysis of randomized controlled trials. Psychosom Med 81 (3)
20. Głąbska D, Guzek D, Groele B, Gutkowska K (2020) Fruit and vegetable intake and mental health in adults: a systematic review. Nutrients 12 (1):115. doi:10.3390/nu12010115
21. Dharmayani PNA, Juergens M, Allman-Farinelli M, Mihrshahi S (2021) Association between fruit and vegetable consumption and depression symptoms in young people and adults aged 15-45: a systematic review of cohort studies. Int J Environ Res Public Health 18 (2). doi:10.3390/ijerph18020780
22. Khalid S, Williams CM, Reynolds SA (2016) Is there an association between diet and depression in children and adolescents? A systematic review. Br J Nutr 116 (12):2097-2108. doi:10.1017/S0007114516004359
23. Wu PY, Chen KM, Belcastro F (2020) Dietary patterns and depression risk in older adults: systematic review and meta-analysis. Nutr Rev. doi:10.1093/nutrit/nuaa118
24. Collins S, Dash S, Allender S, Jacka F, Hoare E (2020) Diet and mental health during emerging adulthood: a systematic review. Emerging Adulthood. doi:10.1177/2167696820943028
25. Bishwajit G, O'Leary DP, Ghosh S, Sanni Y, Shangfeng T, Zhanchun F (2017) Association between depression and fruit and vegetable consumption among adults in South Asia. BMC Psychiatry 17 (1):15-15. doi:10.1186/s12888-017-1198-1
26. McMartin SE, Jacka FN, Colman I (2013) The association between fruit and vegetable consumption and mental health disorders: evidence from five waves of a national survey of Canadians. Prev Med 56 (3-4):225-230. doi:10.1016/j.ypmed.2012.12.016
27. Sanchez-Villegas A, Delgado-Rodriguez M, Alonso A, Schlatter J, Lahortiga F, Serra Majem L, Martinez-Gonzalez MA (2009) Association of the Mediterranean dietary pattern with the incidence of depression: the Seguimiento Universidad de Navarra/University of Navarra follow-up (SUN) cohort. Arch Gen Psychiatry 66 (10):1090-1098. doi:10.1001/archgenpsychiatry.2009.129
28. Mihrshahi S, Dobson AJ, Mishra GD (2015) Fruit and vegetable consumption and prevalence and incidence of depressive symptoms in mid-age women: results from the Australian Longitudinal Study On Women's Health. Eur J Clin Nutr 69 (5):585-591. doi:10.1038/ejcn.2014.222

29. Lee C, Dobson AJ, Brown WJ, Bryson L, Byles J, Warner-Smith P, Young AF (2005) Cohort profile: the Australian Longitudinal Study on Women's Health. Int J Epidemiol 34 (5):987-991. doi:10.1093/ije/dyi098
30. Dobson AJ, Hockey R, Brown WJ, Byles JE, Loxton DJ, McLaughlin D, Tooth LR, Mishra GD (2015) Cohort profile update: Australian Longitudinal Study on Women's Health. Int J Epidemiol 44 (5):1547-1547f. doi:10.1093/ije/dyv110
31. National Health and Medical Research Council (Australia), Australian. Department of Health. (2013) Australian dietary guidelines. https://www.eatforhealth.gov.au/sites/default/files/content/n55_australian_dietary_guidelines.pdf. Accessed 15 March 2021
32. Hodge A, Patterson AJ, Brown WJ, Ireland P, Giles G (2000) The Anti Cancer Council of Victoria FFQ: relative validity of nutrient intakes compared with weighed food records in young to middle-aged women in a study of iron supplementation. Aust N Z J Public Health 24 (6):576-583. doi:10.1111/j.1467-842x.2000.tb00520.x
33. Radloff LS (1977) The CES-D Scale: A self-report depression scale for research in the general population. Applied Psychological Measurement 1 (3):385-401. doi:10.1177/014662167700100306
34. Andresen EM, Malmgren JA, Carter WB, Patrick DL (1994) Screening for depression in well older adults: evaluation of a short form of the CES-D. Am J Prev Med 10 (2):77-84. doi:https://doi.org/10.1016/S0749-3797(18)30622-6
35. Australian Institute of Health and Welfare (2005) Person—tobacco smoking status, code N. Australian Institute of Health and Welfare. https://meteor.aihw.gov.au/content/index.phtml/itemId/270311. Accessed 30 April 2021
36. National Health and Medical Research Council (Australia) (2001) Australian alcohol guidelines: health risks and benefits. Canberra, Australia
37. Brown WJ, Ford JH, Burton NW, Marshall AL, Dobson AJ (2005) Prospective study of physical activity and depressive symptoms in middle-aged women. Am J Prev Med 29 (4):265-272. doi:10.1016/j.amepre.2005.06.009
38. Brown WJ, Burton NW, Marshall AL, Miller YD (2008) Reliability and validity of a modified self-administered version of the Active Australia Physical Activity Survey in a sample of mid-age women. Australian and New Zealand Journal of Public Health 32 (6):535-541. doi:https://doi.org/10.1111/j.1753-6405.2008.00305.x
39. StataCorp (2019) Stata 16 Base Reference Manual. Stata Press, College Station, TX
40. Azur M, Stuart E, Frangakis C, Leaf P (2011) Multiple imputation by chained equations: what is it and how does it work? International Journal of Methods in Psychiatric Research 20:40-49. doi:10.1002/mpr.329
41. Sterne JAC, White IR, Carlin JB, Spratt M, Royston P, Kenward MG, Wood AM, Carpenter JR (2009) Multiple imputation for missing data in epidemiological and clinical research: potential and pitfalls. BMJ 338:b2393. doi:10.1136/bmj.b2393
42. Ocean N, Howley P, Ensor J (2019) Lettuce be happy: A longitudinal UK study on the relationship between fruit and vegetable consumption and well-being. Soc Sci Med 222:335-345. doi:10.1016/j.socscimed.2018.12.017
43. Hoare E, Hockey M, Ruusunen A, Jacka FN (2018) Does Fruit and vegetable consumption during adolescence predict adult depression? A longitudinal study of US adolescents. Front Psychiatry 9:581. doi:10.3389/fpsyt.2018.00581
44. Papier K, Ahmed F, Lee P, Wiseman J (2015) Stress and dietary behaviour among first-year university students in Australia: Sex differences. Nutrition 31 (2):324-330. doi:https://doi.org/10.1016/j.nut.2014.08.004
45. Ansari WE, Adetunji H, Oskrochi R (2014) Food and mental health: relationship between food and perceived stress and depressive symptoms among university students in the United Kingdom. Cent Eur J Public Health 22(2):90-97. doi: 10.21101/cejph.a3941.

46. Mikolajczyk RT, El Ansari W, Maxwell AE (2009) Food consumption frequency and perceived stress and depressive symptoms among students in three European countries. Nutr J 8 (1):31. doi:10.1186/1475-2891-8-31
47. Akbaraly TN, Sabia S, Shipley MJ, Batty GD, Kivimaki M (2013) Adherence to healthy dietary guidelines and future depressive symptoms: evidence for sex differentials in the Whitehall II Study. Am J Clin Nutr 97 (2):419-427. doi:10.3945/ajcn.112.041582
48. Saghafian F, Malmir H, Saneei P, Milajerdi A, Larijani B, Esmaillzadeh A (2018) Fruit and vegetable consumption and risk of depression: accumulative evidence from an updated systematic review and meta-analysis of epidemiological studies. Br J Nutr 119 (10):1087-1101. doi:10.1017/S0007114518000697
49. Liu MW, Chen QT, Towne SD, Jr., Zhang J, Yu HJ, Tang R, Gasevic D, Wang PG, He QQ (2020) Fruit and vegetable intake in relation to depressive and anxiety symptoms among adolescents in 25 low- and middle-income countries. J Affect Disord 261:172-180. doi:10.1016/j.jad.2019.10.007
50. Winpenny EM, van Harmelen AL, White M, van Sluijs EM, Goodyer IM (2018) Diet quality and depressive symptoms in adolescence: no cross-sectional or prospective associations following adjustment for covariates. Public Health Nutr 21 (13):2376-2384. doi:https://dx.doi.org/10.1017/S1368980018001179
51. Kingsbury M, Dupuis G, Jacka F, Roy-Gagnon MH, McMartin SE, Colman I (2016) Associations between fruit and vegetable consumption and depressive symptoms: evidence from a national Canadian longitudinal survey. J Epidemiol Community Health 70 (2):155-161. doi:10.1136/jech-2015-205858
52. Quirk SE, Williams LJ, O'Neil A, Pasco JA, Jacka FN, Housden S, Berk M, Brennan SL (2013) The association between diet quality, dietary patterns and depression in adults: a systematic review. BMC Psychiatry 13. doi:10.1186/1471-244x-13-175.
53. Jacka FN, Cherbuin N, Anstey KJ, Butterworth P (2015) Does reverse causality explain the relationship between diet and depression? J Affect Disord 175:248-250. doi:https://doi.org/10.1016/j.jad.2015.01.007
54. Elstgeest LEM, Visser M, Penninx BWJH, Colpo M, Bandinelli S, Brouwer IA (2019) Bidirectional associations between food groups and depressive symptoms: Longitudinal findings from the Invecchiare in Chianti (InCHIANTI) study. Br J Nutr 121 (4):439-450. doi:10.1017/S0007114518003203
55. Konttinen H, Männistö S, Sarlio-Lähteenkorva S, Silventoinen K, Haukkala A (2010) Emotional eating, depressive symptoms and self-reported food consumption. A population-based study. Appetite 54 (3):473-479. doi:https://doi.org/10.1016/j.appet.2010.01.014
56. Spoor STP, Bekker MHJ, Van Strien T, van Heck GL (2007) Relations between negative affect, coping, and emotional eating. Appetite 48 (3):368-376. doi:https://doi.org/10.1016/j.appet.2006.10.005
57. Rooney C, McKinley MC, Woodside JV (2013) The potential role of fruit and vegetables in aspects of psychological well-being: a review of the literature and future directions. Proc Nutr Soc 72 (4):420-432. doi:10.1017/S0029665113003388
58. Payne ME, Jamerson BD, Potocky CF, Ashley-Koch AE, Speer MC, Steffens DC (2009) Natural food folate and late-life depression. J Nutr Elder 28 (4):348-358. doi:10.1080/01639360903417181
59. Stough C, Scholey A, Lloyd J, Spong J, Myers S, Downey LA (2011) The effect of 90 day administration of a high dose vitamin B-complex on work stress. Human Psychopharmacology: Clinical and Experimental 26 (7):470-476. doi:https://doi.org/10.1002/hup.1229
60. Kennedy DO (2016) B Vitamins and the Brain: Mechanisms, Dose and Efficacy-A Review. Nutrients 8 (2):68-68. doi:10.3390/nu8020068

61. Rao TSS, Asha MR, Ramesh BN, Rao KSJ (2008) Understanding nutrition, depression and mental illnesses. Indian Journal of Psychiatry 50 (2):77-82. doi:10.4103/0019-5545.42391
62. Khosravi M, Sotoudeh G, Amini M, Raisi F, Mansoori A, Hosseinzadeh M (2020) The relationship between dietary patterns and depression mediated by serum levels of folate and vitamin B12. BMC Psychiatry 20 (1):63. doi:10.1186/s12888-020-2455-2
63. Islam MR, Ali S, Karmoker JR, Kadir MF, Ahmed MU, Nahar Z, Islam SMA, Islam MS, Hasnat A, Islam MS (2020) Evaluation of serum amino acids and non-enzymatic antioxidants in drug-naïve first-episode major depressive disorder. BMC Psychiatry 20 (1):333. doi:10.1186/s12888-020-02738-2
64. Jideani AIO, Silungwe H, Takalani T, Omolola AO, Udeh HO, Anyasi TA (2021) Antioxidant-rich natural fruit and vegetable products and human health. International Journal of Food Properties 24 (1):41-67. doi:10.1080/10942912.2020.1866597
65. Brookie KL, Best GI, Conner TS (2018) Intake of raw fruits and vegetables is associated with better mental health than intake of processed fruits and vegetables. Frontiers in Psychology 9:487. doi: 10.3389/fpsyg.2018.00487
66. Baharzadeh E, Siassi F, Qorbani M, Koohdani F, Pak N, Sotoudeh G (2018) Fruits and vegetables intake and its subgroups are related to depression: a cross-sectional study from a developing country. Ann Gen Psychiatry 24 (1):41-67. doi:10.1080/10942912.2020.1866597
67. White IR, Royston P, Wood AM (2011) Multiple imputation using chained equations: issues and guidance for practice. Statistics in Medicine 30 (4):377-399. doi:https://doi.org/10.1002/sim.4067

Table 1. Baseline comparison of characteristics of women who were in the analysis and left out of the analysis due to missing exposure and outcome data (n=4,840)*

Characteristics at baseline (survey 3)	In analysis n = 4,241	Out of analysis* n = 4,840	p-value[a]
Mean age (SD)	27.6 (1.45)	27.6 (1.46)	0.2
CESD-10	6.4 (4.98)	7.5 (5.49)	<0.0001
Sociodemographic variables			
Area of residence			<0.0001
Major cities	58.4%	53.8%	
Inner regional	25.3%	28.4%	
Outer regional/remote/very remote	16.3%	17.8%	
Marital status			<0.0001
Married/ de facto	62.0%	60.8%	
Single	35.5%	34.4%	
Separated/divorced/widowed	2.5%	4.8%	
Education			<0.0001
High school/less	22.4%	36.8%	
Trade/college	23.8%	27.3%	
University	53.8%	35.9%	
Ability to manage income			<0.0001
No difficulty/not too bad	64.6%	52.1%	
Difficult sometimes	26.6%	33.2%	
Very difficult/impossible	8.8%	14.8%	
Having a child			<0.0001
No	75.1%	61.6%	
Yes	24.9%	38.4%	
Health behaviours			
Smoking			<0.0001
Never	62.1%	52.8%	
Ex-smoker	18.6%	18.4%	
Irregular smoker	4.9%	4.8%	
Weekly smoker	2.3%	2.9%	
Daily smoker	12.1%	21.2%	
Physical activity			<0.0001
Nil/sedentary	7.3%	10.8%	
Low	39.2%	39.3%	
Moderate	23.9%	21.7%	
High	29.6%	28.2%	
Alcohol consumption			0.005
Non-drinker	7.0%	9.0%	
Rarely drinks	65.6%	57.1%	
Low-risk drinker	24.4%	29.7%	
Risky/high risk drinker	3.0%	4.2%	
BMI categories			<0.0001
Acceptable weight	61.4%	55.7%	
Underweight	4.2%	4.8%	
Overweight	21.3%	22.8%	
Obese	13.1%	16.8%	

Table 1. *Continued*

Characteristics at baseline (survey 3)	In analysis n = 4,241	Out of analysis* n = 4,840	p-value[a]
History of chronic diseases[b]			0.725
No	97.8%	97.7%	
Yes	2.2%	2.3%	
Fish intake			0.034
Never	7.6%	8.6%	
<30g/day	58.4%	55.9%	
≥30g/day	34.0%	35.5%	

CESD, Center for Epidemiological Studies Depression; SD, standard deviation
* Numbers may vary due to missing values
[a] *p*-values from *t-test* or chi-square test. All statistical tests were conducted using a two-sided 5% level of significance.
[b] Chronic diseases in this study were heart disease, hypertension, diabetes.

Table 2. Distribution of fruit and vegetable consumption at each survey (n= 4,241)

Survey	Survey 3	Survey 4*	Survey 5	Survey 7	Survey 8
Fruit[a]					
≤ 1 serves/day	61.0%	56.9%	57.7%	61.0%	64%
2-3 serves/day	35.5%	39.7%	40.3%	37.5%	34.1%
≥ 4 serves/day	3.5%	3.4%	2.0%	1.5%	1.9%
Vegetables[b]					
≤ 1 serves/day	5.2%	26.1%	2.8%	12.4%	11.6%
2-4 serves/day	80.4%	69.0%	75.9%	75.6%	75.2%
≥ 5 serves/day	14.3%	4.9%	21.3%	12.0%	13.2%
Meet guidelines[c]	7.0%	3.4%	11.6%	6.2%	6.4%

[a] A serve of fruit was equivalent to one medium piece or two small pieces of fruit, or a half cup of diced fruit, berries, or grapes.
[b] A serve of vegetables was equivalent to half a cup (75 g) of cooked vegetables or a cup of salad vegetables.
[c] In the Australian Dietary Guidelines, the minimum recommended daily intake of fruit and vegetables is two serves and five serves respectively for women aged 19–50.
* For survey 4, the response categories for fruit and vegetable were: none, 1, 2–3, 4, and ≥5.

Table 3. Cross-sectional logistic regression models with GEE for associations between fruit and vegetable consumption and depression symptoms on the ALSWH 1973–78 cohort.

	Model 1†		Model 2‡		Model 3§	
	OR	95% CI	OR	95% CI	OR	95% CI
Fruit						
≤ 1 serve/day	1.00	-	1.00	-	1.00	-
2-3 serves/day	**0.85**	**0.79-0.91**	**0.88**	**0.81-0.94**	**0.93**	**0.86-1.00**
≥ 4 serves/day	**0.69**	**0.55-0.86**	**0.71**	**0.56-0.89**	**0.76**	**0.60-0.96**
Vegetables						
≤ 1 serve/day	1.00	-	1.00	-	1.00	-
2-4 serves/day	**0.78**	**0.71-0.86**	**0.81**	**0.73-0.89**	**0.83**	**0.75-0.91**
≥ 5 serves/day	**0.71**	**0.63-0.81**	**0.75**	**0.66-0.86**	**0.79**	**0.69-0.91**

GEE, generalised estimating equations; OR, odds ratio; CI, confidence interval.
Bold indicates a significant association.
† Adjusted for total energy intake and total fish consumption.
‡ Additionally adjusted for sociodemographic variables: area of residence, marital status, education, ability to manage on income, having a child.
§ Additionally adjusted for health behaviours: smoking status, physical activity, alcohol, BMI; and history of chronic disease.

Table 4. Longitudinal logistic regression models with GEE for associations between fruit and vegetable consumption and depression symptoms on the ALSWH 1973-78 cohort.

	Model 1*		Model 2†		Model 3‡		Model 4§	
	OR	95% CI	OR	95% CI	OR	95% CI	OR	95% CI
Fruit								
≤1 serve/day	1.00	-	1.00	-	1.00	-	1.00	-
2-3 serves/day	**0.86**	**0.80-0.93**	**0.86**	**0.79-0.93**	**0.89**	**0.82-0.96**	0.94	0.87-1.02
≥4 serves/day	**0.69**	**0.53-0.89**	**0.68**	**0.53-0.88**	**0.69**	**0.53-0.90**	**0.75**	**0.57-0.97**
Vegetables								
≤1 serve/day	1.00	-	1.00	-	1.00	-	1.00	-
2-4 serves/day	**0.79**	**0.72-0.88**	**0.79**	**0.71-0.88**	**0.82**	**0.74-0.91**	**0.85**	**0.76-0.95**
≥5 serves/day	**0.72**	**0.63-0.84**	**0.72**	**0.62-0.83**	**0.76**	**0.66-0.88**	**0.81**	**0.70-0.94**

GEE, generalised estimating equations; OR, odds ratio; CI, confidence interval.
Bold indicates a significant association.
* Adjusted for history of depression.
† Additionally adjusted for total energy intake and total fish consumption.
‡ Additionally adjusted for sociodemographic variables: area of residence, marital status, education, ability to manage on income, having a child.
§ Additionally adjusted for health behaviours: smoking status, physical activity, alcohol, BMI, and history of chronic disease.

Further information

The current study focused on Australian women who were born between 1973 and 1978. The data were drawn from the Australian Longitudinal Study on Women's Health, which comprises four cohorts. Although younger cohort (1989–95 cohort) data is available, this study only analysed data from the 1973–78 cohort because they had been followed throughout their young adulthood (18-44 years), which is the age range of the target population in the current book. As mentioned in the limitations of the study, the distribution of fruit and vegetable presented in Table 2 cannot be directly compared for each survey because the questions and response options are inconsistent across the surveys (Appendix B: Supplementary table 1). Total energy intakes were available in survey 3 and 5; however in the current analysis, only data from Survey 5 was included in the modelling because the recent dietary intake was collected in this survey.

Despite long-term follow up, missing data commonly occurs in longitudinal studies within a wave or a full-wave, particularly in population-based studies. Several simulation studies have compared the performance of the complete case analysis with multiple imputation methods for handling missing data in longitudinal studies.(10-12) Although it is considered reasonable to impute missing outcome variables, it may introduce additional complexity with the data and make the implementation more challenging.(10) Therefore, the current study focused on missingness in the covariates, whereas the outcome is fully observed to perform multiple imputation under missing at random assumption. This approach resulted in smaller standard errors and a less restrictive missingness mechanism.

References

1. Vos T, Lim SS, Abbafati C, Abbas KM, Abbasi M, Abbasifard M, et al. Global burden of 369 diseases and injuries in 204 countries and territories, 1990-2019: a systematic analysis for the Global Burden of Disease Study 2019. The Lancet. 2020;396(10258):1204-22.
2. Salk RH, Hyde JS, Abramson LY. Gender differences in depression in representative national samples: meta-analyses of diagnoses and symptoms. Psychol Bull. 2017;143(8):783-822.
3. Sloan DM, Sandt AR. Gender differences in depression. Women's Health. 2006;2(3):425-34.
4. Boyd A, Van de Velde S, Vilagut G, de Graaf R, O'Neill S, Florescu S, et al. Gender differences in mental disorders and suicidality in Europe: Results from a large cross-sectional population-based study. J Affect Disord. 2015;173:245-54.
5. Cho MJ, Kim J-K, Jeon HJ, Suh T, Chung I-W, Hong JP, et al. Lifetime and 12-month prevalence of DSM-IV psychiatric disorders among Korean adults. The Journal of Nervous and Mental Disease. 2007;195(3).
6. Akbaraly TN, Sabia S, Shipley MJ, Batty GD, Kivimaki M. Adherence to healthy dietary guidelines and future depressive symptoms: evidence for sex differentials in the Whitehall II Study. Am J Clin Nutr. 2013;97(2):419-27.
7. Hoare E, Hockey M, Ruusunen A, Jacka FN. Does Fruit and vegetable consumption during adolescence predict adult depression? A longitudinal study of US adolescents. Front Psychiatry. 2018;9:581.
8. Chang SC, Cassidy A, Willett WC, Rimm EB, O'Reilly EJ, Okereke OI. Dietary flavonoid intake and risk of incident depression in midlife and older women. Am J Clin Nutr. 2016;104(3):704-14.
9. Mihrshahi S, Dobson AJ, Mishra GD. Fruit and vegetable consumption and prevalence and incidence of depressive symptoms in mid-age women: results from the Australian Longitudinal Study On Women's Health. Eur J Clin Nutr. 2015;69(5):585-91.
10. Huque MH, Carlin JB, Simpson JA, Lee KJ. A comparison of multiple imputation methods for missing data in longitudinal studies. BMC Medical Research Methodology. 2018;18(1):168.
11. Karahalios A, Baglietto L, Lee KJ, English DR, Carlin JB, Simpson JA. The impact of missing data on analyses of a time-dependent exposure in a longitudinal cohort: a simulation study. Emerg Themes Epidemiol. 2013;10(1):6-.
12. Young R, Johnson DR. Handling missing values in longitudinal panel data with multiple imputation. J Marriage Fam. 2015;77(1):277-94.

Chapter 4: Discussion and Conclusion

This chapter discusses the findings and provides the conclusion of the study. It begins by providing key findings and a summary from the systematic review and secondary analysis study. Then, it is followed by a discussion of the contribution of the study to the literature. The next section considers the strengths and limitations of the study. Finally, the possible future directions for research based on the collective findings are outlined.

This book examined the association between fruit and vegetable consumption by conducting a systematic review and a secondary analysis from the 1973–78 cohort of the ALSWH. The first study (Chapter 2) systematically reviewed the existing literature evaluating the association between fruit and vegetable consumption and depression symptoms in young people and adults aged 15-45 using longitudinal methods. The second study (Chapter 3) examined the differential effects of fruit and vegetables in relation to depression symptoms over a 15-year follow-up in the 1973–78 cohort of the ALSWH.

Key findings from this research

- There is a potential association between higher consumption of fruit and vegetable and lower risk of depression symptoms in young people and adults, among women in particular.
- There is generally low intakes of fruit and vegetables in young people and adults

Summary of systematic review findings

The first study aimed to systematically review longitudinal studies that evaluated the association between fruit and vegetable consumption and depression symptoms in young people and adults aged 15–45. A total of 12 longitudinal studies were identified from seven countries and included in the qualitative synthesis. Most studies (five of six studies) reported that fruit consumption was inversely associated with depression symptoms. Fewer studies (two of five studies) found an inverse association between vegetable consumption and depression symptoms. With regards to combined consumption, two of six studies showed that total fruit and vegetable intake was associated with a lower risk of depression. Although the results across studies vary due to differences in measurements, sample sizes and statistical analysis, the evidence seems to be building a potential protective role of fruit and vegetable consumption on depression symptoms.

Summary of the 1973–78 cohort of the ALSWH findings

The second study aimed to examine the differential effects of fruit and vegetables in relation to depression symptoms over a 15-year follow-up in the 1973–78 cohort of the ALSWH. In cross-sectional analysis, fruit and vegetables were associated with lower odds of depression symptoms. In the longitudinal analysis, higher consumption of fruit (≥ 4 servings) and vegetables (≥ 2 servings) was also consistently associated with lower odds of depression symptoms compared with consuming one serve or less of fruit and vegetables. Therefore, the results provide further evidence that higher consumption of fruit and vegetables is inversely associated with depression symptoms.

Contribution of the two studies to the literature

The role of fruit and vegetables on depression has been a growing area of research over the past few decades. A limited number of reviews have been conducted to evaluate the relationship between fruit and vegetable consumption and mental health,[1, 2] particularly depression.[3] However, most included studies in the systematic reviews have used cross-sectional designs, which have some limitations. In this book, young adults aged 15-45 are the target population because this is a life stage where key life transitions occur, and their health behaviours may change. To date, there is no systematic review evaluating the association between fruit and vegetable consumption and depression symptoms in this age group.

In Chapter 2, the systematic review evaluated the findings of this association from a total of 12 longitudinal studies. It restricted the study design to longitudinal design because it allows observing the direction of change over time in particular individuals within the cohort.(4) This study has reviewed the findings and presented the combined and separated consumption of fruit and vegetables in relation to depression symptoms to observe any differential effects. It showed more evidence that fruit consumption was significantly associated with a lower risk of depression symptoms in young people and adults aged 15-45, while vegetable consumption tended to have mixed results.

As discussed in Chapter 1, some existing studies have observed gender differences in depression.(5-8) Interestingly, the current systematic review also observed the potential of gender differences between fruit and vegetable consumption and depression symptoms. Although some of the included studies showed a weak association, an inverse association was more likely to be observed among women than men. A recent study from the National Longitudinal Survey of Youth 1979 for Children and Young Adults confirmed that gender moderated the association between fruit consumption and depression among young adults.(9) Additionally, young women were more likely to consume healthy food, which comprised fruit and vegetables, than young men.(9)

In alignment with this finding, the secondary analysis study in Chapter 3 supports the evidence that higher consumption of fruit and vegetables is significantly associated with a lower risk of depression symptoms among young Australian women. However, some previous studies have had mixed results in the association between fruit and vegetable consumption and depression in women. For example, the Whitehall II prospective cohort study from the UK found that maintaining and improving vegetable intake is significantly associated with a lower risk of recurrent depressive symptoms over a 10-year follow-up, but not in fruit.(10) Conversely, findings from the 1946-51 cohort of ALSWH in Australia found that higher consumption of fruit is significantly associated with a lower risk of depressive symptoms over a 6-year follow-up, but it was unclear in vegetables.(11) It is worth noting that both studies highlight that fruit (10) and vegetables (11) have possible protective effects because there was an inverse association even though it was a weak association.

In terms of fruit and vegetable consumption trends, some literature in Chapter 1 reported low fruit and vegetable consumption in young adults. Findings provided in Chapter 2 and 3 also confirm that few young adults consume fruit and vegetables following the daily recommended intakes at a national level. In the 1973-78 cohort of the ALSWH, for instance, between 3.4% to 11.6% of Australian women consumed fruit and vegetable following Australian guidelines during their young adulthood. A longitudinal study identifying individual and socio-environmental factors in fruit and vegetable consumption in young adulthood found favourable taste preferences, home food availability (including unhealthy food, fruit and vegetables), and partners healthy eating attitudes were significant predictors of fruit and vegetable intake.(12) In relation to home food availability, parental support for healthy eating plays a vital role in fruit and vegetable consumption in young women and men.(13) Life-course transitions, commonly occur during emerging adulthood, such as becoming a full-time employee,(14) leaving the parental home and leaving education(14, 15) have contributed to change in diet. For example, leaving the parental home was associated with decreased fruit and vegetable consumption in young adults aged 14–30.(15) Generally, young adults living on their own for the first time are more likely to have poor dietary intake due to food costs, availability and preparation.(16, 17) Therefore, it is essential to develop strategies in increasing the daily intake of fruit and vegetable during emerging adulthood.

Both studies in this book provide an important insight into the role of diet and particularly fruit and vegetables in the development of depression in young adults and contribute additional knowledge to the research base on this topic in this population. This study helps fill a gap in the research around the diet-depression relationship. Taken together, these findings suggest the role of fruit and vegetable in lowering depression symptoms in young people and adults, among women in particular.

Strengths and limitation

There are several strengths of this book. Firstly, the unique aspect of this book focuses on the association between fruit and vegetable consumption and depression symptoms in young adults.

This particular population has experienced most key life transitions, which may change their dietary habits and make them more susceptible to depression. In addition, the exclusive use of longitudinal study design in the first study provides a clearer direction of this association and minimise the reverse causality. The majority of the included studies in the systematic review and the secondary analysis study using the 1973–78 cohort of the ALSWH have large sample size that offer greater precision and easier to assess the representativeness of the sample. Another strength of the secondary analysis study is the use of data from a prospective cohort with repeated measurements over 15 years.

Some limitations must be considered in interpreting the study findings. Differences in the measurement of fruit and vegetable intake and assessment of depression across the included studies in the systematic review may distort the results because each instrument has a different way to define the variable. Another limitation from the systematic review is that the age ranges in most studies were slightly extended outside our target population. It is recognised that a large number of participants in the 1973–78 cohort of ALSWH had missing data in fruit and vegetable intake and the CESD-10 score. Additionally, the exclusion of survey 6 from the analysis may change the direction of the odds of depression symptoms towards the null. Reverse causality in the secondary analysis study exists due to its observational nature. Both studies in this book also note that the use of self-reported reports may introduce recall bias.

Future research directions

The two studies in this book add to the body of research supporting fruit and vegetables as a protective factor against depression symptoms in young people and adults. It is worth noting that some limitations should be addressed to provide more robust evidence in this field.

Gender differences

Although potential gender differences were observed in the current systematic review, the current study could not provide a definitive conclusion due to the lack of longitudinal studies.

More longitudinal studies with population-based samples are required to examine possible gender differences in diet and depression in young adulthood.

Differences in assessment of depression

A variety of depression assessment instruments are available to determine whether an individual has depression symptoms. However, each instrument has different ways of scoring and cut-off points. To address this issue, clinician assessments or antidepressant prescriptions are recommended along with a self-reported depression scale to define depression or depression symptoms for future studies.

Differences in measurement of fruit and vegetable intake

Fruit and vegetables are commonly reported based on portions or servings in daily intake. It is important to mention a difference between portion and serving size, yet both sizes have a standard size in gram. Using gram (g) for analysis purposes should be considered to standardise the measurement and provide the range of the quantity of fruit and vegetables that should be eaten to obtain its benefit for mental health.

Reverse causality

Although positive results have been observed in the association between fruit and vegetable consumption and depression symptoms, as discussed in Chapter 2 and 3, it should be noted that reverse causation exists in the diet-depression relationship. It has been acknowledged that this limitation is a predominant challenge to elucidate this relationship. Replication of the results in other populations is highly needed to gain confidence in study findings in this field. More cohort and intervention studies are warranted to elucidate the causal role of fruit and vegetables in the development of depression symptoms.

Implications for the prevention of depression

Generally, the findings seem to be consistent with previous studies that young people and adults are particularly susceptible to depression and less likely to consume daily fruit and vegetables following the recommended guidelines. The results presented in this book reflect that there is the potential for increased fruit and vegetable consumption to reduce risk of depression symptoms in young people and adults. The plausible mechanisms through which fruit and vegetables can reduce depression symptoms have yet to be fully established. However, some pathways have been proposed, including the role of fruit and vegetables in the synthesis of neurotransmitters.(18, 19) The main finding that increased fruit and vegetable intake has the potential to reduce the risk of depression needs to be confirmed using a more rigorous study design such as a cluster randomised trial where the role of diet in the prevention of depressive symptoms can be further elucidated.

A meta-analysis evaluating the efficacy of dietary interventions on depression symptoms and anxiety indicated that these interventions had promising positive effects on depression symptoms in non-clinical samples.(20) Although the majority of interventions primarily targeted weight loss, the results also showed a significant reduction in depression symptoms.(20)

Additionally, a preliminary study suggested that a 12-week dietary support intervention resulted in significantly lower costs to the health sector and societal perspectives based on a formal economic evaluation.(21) This indicates that changes in diet by increasing fruit and vegetable intake may be a cost-effective intervention for reducing the risk of depression.

Further behavioural research on how individuals make decisions about their diet throughout their young adulthood period is needed to understand how to encourage them to increase daily consumption of fruit and vegetables. Population-targeted dietary interventions may bring larger benefits for reducing the burden of depression at a lower cost to society. Increasing support and investment in dietary interventions to reduce depression symptoms have the potential to improve general mental health status. Indeed, dietary modification may benefit physical health and psychological well-being and offer the potential for meaningful public health impact.

Conclusion and contribution to policy, practice, and research

The collective findings from this book suggest a potentially important role of fruit and vegetables in reducing the risk of depression symptoms in young people and adults and that dietary interventions, which include increasing fruit and vegetable consumption, are a promising preventive intervention to reduce the burden of depression. Given positive findings in this book, future longitudinal studies should consider whether there are differential effects of raw and processed (e.g. frozen, canned) fruit and vegetable in relation to depression symptoms in this population.

Because of the low adherence rates to dietary guidelines for fruit and vegetables among young people and adults, nutrition campaigns and interventions should be targeted at these populations. Communicating the potential benefits of fruit and vegetables in relation to lowering the risk of depression symptoms may be an effective strategy for increasing fruit and vegetable consumption in young adults and people. Particularly aiming at young women, the perceived benefits of healthy eating were positively associated with higher fruit and vegetable consumption.(13) To do so, the findings from this book have been disseminated to a broader audience on relevant channels, such as social media and online news (Appendix C).

Furthermore, policy actions at a national and international level are needed to increase the availability, acceptability and affordability of fruit and vegetables. Several interventions that have been conducted and have positive outcomes to increase fruit and vegetables should be considered, such as the availability of community gardens,(22) mobile fruit and vegetable markets(23). Price reductions on fruit and vegetables may be an effective strategy to increase purchasing of healthy foods in a community-based setting.

CPSIA information can be obtained
at www.ICGtesting.com
Printed in the USA
BVHW050003280623
666449BV00016B/833